PAUSE *in* WONDER

"Many years ago Deacon Eddie Ensley's book *Sounds of Wonder* was a great inspiration to me. He has continued to mature in age and spirituality since those early days. His new book, *Pause in Wonder*, wonderfully represents that growth."

John Michael Talbot
Singer-songwriter, speaker, and author of *Lessons from a Troubadour*

"*Pause in Wonder* offers a personal and compelling sharing of loss, pain, and grief. This story is a wonderful bridge-builder and a journey of hope and joy especially for our native brothers and sisters searching for their roots who face shame for their identity. This book points to an enculturated approach to find your true self with scripture, family history, prayer, and poetry."

Sr. Kateri Mitchell
Founder of The Tekakwitha Conference

"*Pause in Wonder* is beautifully written, honest, tender, and uplifting. I loved especially Deacon Eddie Ensley's candid sharing about his own struggles, his descriptions of the beauty of nature, and his anecdotes about his grandparents and his Native American heritage. His life bears witness to the fact that the gospel expresses itself in the cultures of various peoples, while those cultures are also purified and restored in Christ."

Mary Healy
Professor of sacred scripture at Sacred Heart Major Seminary

"Deacon Eddie Ensley is a master storyteller. By humbly sharing stories from his own journey with God, he shows how one can enter intimacy with the Lord in a multitude of ways and experience his healing, love, care, joy, and goodness. May *Pause in Wonder* be a source to awaken joy and wonder for all who read its pages."

Dan Almeter
Counselor and pastoral leader of Alleluia Christian Community

"Deacon Eddie Ensley skillfully blends testimony, teaching, and storytelling to share his own fascinating journey with the Lord. He has had quite an adventure! Ensley witnesses in a touching way how the Lord has used his very brokenness and limitations to 'work everything to the good' in his life. *Pause in Wonder* is singularly interesting and instructive—a rewarding read!"

Patti Gallagher Mansfield
Author of *As by a New Pentecost*

"One of the biggest lies many of us accept each day is that joy is a reaction to external circumstances. In reality, true joy comes from within and flows from the power of Holy Spirit. In *Pause in Wonder*, Deacon Eddie Ensley and Deacon Robert Herrmann remind us that we can experience joy anytime and anywhere, even in the midst of suffering. As they so powerfully point out, joy is a choice. If you're looking to find greater joy in your life, start by choosing to read this book. You won't regret it!"

Gary Zimak
Catholic speaker, radio host, and author of *Give Up Worry For Lent!*

PAUSE *in* WONDER

Learning to Delight in God and His World

Deacon Eddie Ensley *with*
Deacon Robert Herrmann

AVE MARIA PRESS AVE Notre Dame, Indiana

Founded in 1865, Ave Maria Press is a ministry of the United States Province of Holy Cross.

www.avemariapress.com

Paperback: ISBN-13 978-1-59471-955-4

E-book: ISBN-13 978-1-59471-956-1

Cover image © AVTG/iStock/Getty Images Plus.

Cover design by Andrew Wagoner.

Text design by Christopher D. Tobin.

Printed and bound in the United States of America.

Library of Congress Cataloging-in-Publication Data is available.

Pause in Wonder is dedicated to two spiritual
friends of the authors,
Joanna Brunson and Martin Wolf;
and to two friends of Deacon Ensley from the Alleluia
Community whose prayers helped beyond measure,
Dan Almeter and Chuck Hornsby.
And for Deacon Ensley's beloved high school French
teacher, Emma Jayne Kretlow,
who was his first model of what it means
to be a good Catholic.

Inculturation elevates and fulfills. Certainly, we should esteem the indigenous mysticism that sees the interconnection and interdependence of the whole of creation, the mysticism of gratuitousness that loves life as a gift, the mysticism of a sacred wonder before nature and all its forms of life.

—Francis, *Querida Amazonia (Beloved Amazon)*, 73

Contents

Introduction

EMBRACING JOY

Only the heart that hurts has a right to joy.
—Lewis Smedes

And the ransomed of the Lord shall return,
and enter Zion singing,
crowned with everlasting joy;
They meet with joy and gladness,
sorrow and mourning flee away.
—Isaiah 35:10

Beneath the clutter of everyday busyness and discouragement that we may often feel, there is a yearning. Sometimes it is quiet, hardly noticeable. Sometimes it throbs like a toothache. This yearning is built into the very cells of our bodies and inhabits the textures of our souls. It is the quest for joy. Our finite world is bordered by the infinite, a limitless horizon that sometimes invades and draws us close as it gladdens us. Those invasions of wonderment and mystery, those graced moments, can sneak up on us unexpectedly and awe us into a deep joy.

Perhaps you are walking along the beach. You cease to be aware of the movement of your muscles or the splashing of your feet in the water. The sound of the breaking waves stills

and calms your mind. You seem one with the sea, the beach.
You feel connected. Your fears leave you for a moment, and
the wonderment of sacred mystery rushes in, closer to you
than the blood that surges through your veins. As the freshness of the world astonishes you, as you catapult into joy.
Deep down, you experience the sentiment of Psalm 98:1,
"O sing to the LORD a new song, for he has done wonderful
things . . ." (NASB).

In the scriptures, the words *wonder* and *joy* are often
used interchangeably; they are part of the same experience.
We pause and the freshness of God and his world brings the
wonderment of joy. Wonder and joy are beyond any logical
definition. They are bathed in the mystery that is God. In this
book we use them nearly interchangeably. They are invoked
more than defined. Right now I want us to see this through
the lens of joy. The first chapter will focus more on the lens
of wonder and awe.

Perhaps that joy is more subdued. You have grieved deeply for weeks over the death of a loved one, then as you are
attempting to pray through the sorrow you pause and realize
you still have God. You can find a way, hard as it is, to live
and love again.

Joy comes in other, more traditional ways too: while you
are reading the Bible, receiving Communion, or voicing
praise. These times tantalize us, tease us, and make us hungry
for more. They put us in touch with our capacity for wonder
and awe. They inspire us to pause in wonder, to delight in
every possible way in the goodness of the Lord.

Sadly, there are also times when the joy seems to fizzle and
fade, eluding us at every turn. Where has it gone? And more
importantly, how can we recapture it? We will never find joy
in accumulated possessions, or in superficial interactions, or

even in the deeds we accomplish. All we have to do to know this is true is to look at the lives of those who have all these things.

God Is Our Source of Wonder and Joy

In the scriptures we find wonder and joy closely knit together. Take a look at Psalm 65:9, "Distant peoples stand in awe of your marvels; the places of morning and evening you make resound with joy."

There is only one sure source of joy: God himself. In the New Testament, joy is a part of God's very being, and his Spirit manifests this heavenly joy in his children. "The fruit of the Spirit is love, joy, peace, patience, kindness, generosity, faithfulness" (Gal 5:22). "In spite of persecution you received the word with joy inspired by the Holy Spirit" (1 Thes 1:6, NRSV:CE). Joy is the deep-down sense of well-being and fullness that abides in the heart of the person touched by God. Joy is something very deep and profound, something that affects the entire personality.

God's gift of joy does not take away all sorrow and difficulty. We all have loss, sadness, and those times when the rug is pulled from beneath our feet. Part of the pathway to joy is learning to grieve and facing the lessons we need to learn.

When Joy and Sorrow Meet

We can easily think of joy when all goes well. It is much harder to find joy in times of sorrow: Standing at the grave as a deacon or priest says final prayers. Holding the hand of a friend whose child has disappeared into a fog of drugs, or has died through some random violence. Reeling from the news that you have been laid off from the job that supported your family for thirty years. Hurting from the loss of a lifelong friend who stops speaking to you, seemingly without reason.

Is joy really possible in such a mixed-up world? How can faith help you in the midst of these sorrows? God assures us that even in our sorrows we can find joy, genuine joy. This is no fake joy in which we soft-pedal and deny the harsh realities of life, plastering on a syrupy smile and saying, "Now let's all just be happy." Rather, it is the summons from God to pause and acknowledge his presence, to take to heart Paul's admonition to "rejoice, again I say rejoice" (Phil 4:4). In choosing joy at every stage of our lives—in the low periods of life as well as in the heights—we acknowledge our total dependence, and his unfailing love.

By choosing joy, we do not deny the reality of suffering. The only healthy response to pain and sadness is to face reality head-on. God wants to walk with us *through* the valley of the shadow of death, not around it. He wants to walk with us even in those moments when we cannot feel him near because of the intensity of our grief. Yet his presence is real, while the valley is merely a shadow.

And aren't you glad it is just a shadow? Sorrow can knit us to God, deepening our relationship and connection to him, if only we will pause and attune the ears of the heart.

Scripture tells us, "When troubles of any kind come your way, consider it an opportunity for great joy" (Jas 1:2–4, NLT). The Eastern Churches have a phrase, "joy-making sorrow." The truth of faith is that our sorrows can make rich compost for joy, but if hope is to grow out of our sorrow, it will be because our sorrow drives us to God. When sorrow does this, it disowns its own essence, and points us in its opposite direction. When sorrow helps us to view God, it clears away the thick trees, and lets the sunlight into the forest shadows.

Joy is nothing less than the brightness that illuminates God's face, wonderment beyond all wonderment; in order to see that brightness, we must look at him, let his love clasp us even in the rock-bottoms of life. Our hearts are built to enshrine God. The very fabric of our being was created to be his homestead, and we can enshrine God in sorrowful times as well as joyful ones. In the wondrous conception of John the Baptist, barrenness was changed to delight. In the coming of Jesus in Mary's womb, joy transfigured the entire world's sorrow. The child born that first Christmas came to transfigure our personal sorrows into joy also.

The greatest gladness we will ever have is God. Like the infant John the Baptist leaping with joy in the womb, God wants to pass on to each of us, regardless of our age, the delight of being a child of an all-loving Father.

We too can leap with astonishment that God has come and can wondrously rearrange us, so like Mary we can contain him whom the whole world cannot contain. We can breathe God, love others, and manifest God's joy in the very fibers of our being. Throughout this whole book we can learn to praise, worship, and rejoice in the One who makes all things new.

God alone can still the tumult of our emotions and quench our thirst for the immortal. Only God can go into the depths of our souls and, from his throne, flood our nature with contentment. The deeper the sorrow, the more striking the inner joy. Joy that springs from sorrow is joy that will last.

In the Gospel of John, Jesus comforts his followers, "So you also are now in anguish. But I will see you again, and your hearts will rejoice, and no one will take your joy away from you" (Jn 16:22). "Until now you have not asked anything in my name; ask and you will receive, so that your joy will be complete "(Jn 16:24). His voice resounds through the scriptures, he touches us intimately in the Eucharist, and he caresses us with forgiveness in the Sacrament of Reconciliation.

Every morning, when we wake up, we have twenty-four brand-new hours to live. When we pause enough to view the beauty of God's creation, both within and without, the Holy Spirit can flood our souls. The mere sense of living in a creation that reflects the Creator can be an amazement when we allow God to be a part of it. That amazement roots us in joy. You feel like breaking into joyful song, like this: "They who dwell in the ends of the earth stand in awe of Your signs; You make the dawn and the sunset shout for joy" (Ps 65:8, NASB).

The word in the original Greek New Testament that is used for joy is *chara*, which means "joy" and "rejoice." It is related to the word *charis,* which means "grace." It is a Greek noun that describes a feeling of inner wonderment, delight, or rejoicing. Joy in the New Testament is virtually always used to signify a feeling of exuberance and solace that is based on spiritual realities and independent of what happens. It is an inner gladness, a deep-seated pleasure. It is a depth of assurance and confidence that ignites a cheerful heart that leads to cheerful behavior. Joy is not an experience that comes from advantageous circumstances, but is God's gift.

Happiness and Joy

Though the two words have much in common, and we often use them interchangeably, I think most of us know intuitively that there is a distinction between happiness and joy. Both are positive emotions, but there is a difference: While happiness depends on our circumstances, joy is rooted in something solid. Happiness happens, but joy abides. I take a holiday and make a trip I have always wanted to make; happiness fills me up. But then the day comes when I must go back to work, and

I am let down. You may have a great Thanksgiving meal with extended family and you happily talk about old times, but then later in the day hidden tension between family members erupts in old arguments never won, and you are sad.

Happiness is often unpredictable, like a boat with no anchor struggling through tossing waves. Joy is different. It runs deeper. I was joyful at my baptism when I was twelve and flowing over with joy at my ordination seventeen years ago when family and friends came from everywhere to witness it. As Ransomed Heart women's ministry leader Stasi Eldredge has said, "Joy is not happiness on steroids."[1] We all can feel happiness at certain times in our lives; joy roots itself in something different.

Joy has its tendrils in God. It draws on the infinity of his love. It is a matter of relationship with the wellspring of joy and is not due to our circumstances. God is always available, always ready to touch us. The question becomes: Are we willing to touch him? Do we want to seek deep joy in our lives?

The journey into God, with God, is a journey that changes how the world seems to us. As God floods our hearts, we see the world with new eyes, shimmering with his presence. The embrace of a loved one, a sunset, spring water flowing over rocks, and the wonder in a toddler's eyes surprise us, and reality takes on a new splendor.

Brother Lawrence, seventeenth-century author of *The Practice of the Presence of God,* wrote of a time of his awakening to God's joy:

> Natural objects were glorified. My spiritual vision was so clarified that I saw beauty in every material object in the universe. The woods were vocal with heavenly music. Oh, how I was changed! Everything became new. My horses and hogs and

everybody became changed! When I went in the morning into the fields to work . . . the glory of God appeared in all His visible creation. I well remember we reaped oats, and how every straw and head of the oats seemed, as it were, arrayed in a kind of rainbow glory, or to glow, if I may so express it, in the glory of God.[2]

The words *joy* and *joyful* are used a total of seventy times in the New Testament. The gospels portray Jesus as being full of joy, of really enjoying meals with his friends and even outcasts and sinners. We also are called to partake of that joy. But how? How can we live a more joy-filled life? That is the question addressed in this book.

This book presents practical pathways of experiencing joy, ways so simple and so obvious that we easily overlook them. As you learn about the gladness God offers and as you increasingly open your heart to the loving mystery of God and choose the bright gladness that is God himself, you will more and more learn to love the people around you. A fresh joy will root itself deep in the cellar of your soul. As the new love and life within you help you to spend yourself for God, others, and the poor, you can begin to say with St. Paul, "It is no longer I who live, but it is Christ who lives in me" (Gal 2:20, NRSV:CE).

About Spiritual Journaling

Each chapter in this book ends with journal starters that were created by Deacon Robert Herrmann. For this chapter, I asked Deacon Robert to write a brief introduction about spiritual journaling, and to share with you a bit of his story. Here is what he wrote!

———————

I HAVE KEPT A JOURNAL SINCE I WAS SIXTEEN. That may seem young to start a spiritual journal, but a teenage brush with the law greatly accelerated the urgency with which I set out upon my spiritual pilgrimage. I was caught in the company of a friend who was shoplifting. The only real punishment was seeing the profound disappointment in my parents' eyes when they picked me up at the police station.

That evening, in my shame and confusion, I was met by the unexpected grace of God. As I lay in bed, weeping over the day's events, the heavy weight that had been bearing down on me began to lift. Something I could not explain or control began to wash my spirit and mind. While I heard no voice and saw no lights flashing from the sky, an unmistakable presence of joy and love enveloped me, a love that seeped into every aching cell of my body. God began to touch every shadow of despair inhabiting my mind; his love began to fill me with an inner warmth and brilliance.

I didn't understand how I could feel joyful at that point, but what was happening inside of me was out of my hands. Despite the shame, my body rattled with an unexpected gladness. In the midst of what would have been the worst night of my life, God touched my soul and his sheer presence was my abounding joy. I picked up an empty composition book I had handy and wrote what had just transpired in my soul.

Hope and joy put me to sleep that night. As I reflect on that night now, I believe I knew that my life had just turned a corner. What the experience meant has taken years to unfold. I had a deep desire for long periods of quiet, contemplative prayer, though I didn't know the word *contemplative* at the time. I wanted to rest in quietness in the presence of the One who had touched my heart and turned my life around.

I began to reprioritize my days so I could have time for prayer—sometimes an hour or two or more every day. A riot of powerful, wondrous sensations streamed through me. I had no one to listen to what was happening inside me. I needed to tell someone of these experiences. I soon found my composition book to be a therapist, spiritual advisor, friend, and place to celebrate the wondrous new reality in my soul. I simply wrote out whatever was going on inside me, somehow knowing God was listening, that this was a form of prayer.

Over time, this spiritual journal contained all kinds of notations. I wrote out my prayers. I sketched pictures to symbolize my feelings. I penned hymns of joy and poured out my fears. The book soon filled with poems, pictures, and prayers. All the bewildering newness of an adolescent spiritual awakening was sorted out in that journal.

One of the things I paid special attention to was journaling about joy. I discovered that the simple joy of feeling the sun beat down on me was enshrined in my journal. The gladness of smelling rain hit the ground amplified when I wrote about it.

I have kept a journal ever since. Journaling has helped seal and deepen not only my encounter with God but also my joys. My journaling became a means of seeing my inner reality clearly and taking the whole of that inner reality to a loving God for transformation. In this way, journaling brought about much of my own healing, as I uncovered the plot of my life, and continued to process those experiences.

It is my prayer that, as you learn to practice this form of spiritual discipline, spiritual journaling will also help you to capture the impressions and experiences that you have in your prayer time. You don't need any fancy equipment—just a simple notepad and pen will do. Choose a special time each day to find a comfortable place to sit and think, and ask God to show you where he was present in your life that day. Then write down your thoughts as they come to you—don't try to censor yourself or write for an audience. No one needs to see what you have written but you and God.

Journaling starts an inner process. Your problems begin to untangle and your soul unfurls. You can never predict what you'll run into once the process gets going. Your writing will come from your memories, your dreams, your prayers, and rejoicing.

Much of your journaling will call you to remember, and in that experience of remembering, you will bump into the surprising presence of God and see your past in a different light.

And now . . . let us begin that journey together! Let us take a few moments to sit in silence, to learn how to pause in wonder.

One

ON TIPTOE WITH AWE

I wonder as I wander out under the sky,
How Jesus the Savior did come for to die,
For poor lowly people like you and like I,
I wonder as I wander, . . . out under the sky.
—JOHN JACOB NILES, TRADITIONAL APPALACHIAN
CHRISTMAS CAROL

One of the main components in joy is wonder.

When I think of wonder I think of my Cherokee Indian grandfather, Pop. A baptized Christian, he held on to the values of his Native culture and the Bible Granny used to read to him. He lived in a small cottage on a high bluff overlooking the stunningly beautiful Chattahoochee River. Pop would often take long walks along the bluff and through the woods, sometimes shaking his gourd shaker. He would sit or stand along the river, then slowly take in all he saw.

Once I asked him, "What are you doing, Pop?"

"I'm looking at what is in front of me."

"Why?" I probed. "Why are you looking at what's in front of you?"

"Because," he said, "when you look long enough, it shimmers, and you see the glory." Pop experienced wonder and awe in all of nature. He taught me, by his example, to do the same.

The Joy of Wonder

Wonder is a beautiful, mysterious thing. God wants us to marvel and find joy in him and what he has created. Such moments overtake us at times—we can neither pick nor control these moments. They simply awe us into a fullness of joy.

Think of a time you were outside, spending a moment in nature. You looked out over a huge seascape that was too vast to take in, and your heart beat with joy at the thought that God is infinitely vaster. Or perhaps you stood under the canopy of a night sky peppered with stars and remembered that the One who stretched them out over the universe also made and cares for you.

Maybe you can recall holding your infant and looking into big round eyes as he or she marveled at the world. Maybe you are thinking of a scripture verse, a painting, or a poem. Or perhaps you remember a time when you were with a group of longtime friends and the conversation ceased because no more needed to be said.

What are you thinking of? What is it that overtakes you with a wordless joy as you marvel at an enduring human love that is so like God's love?

When we pause to wonder and stand in awe, finding joy in the seemingly inexplicable, we are bathed in what many Native cultures call the "Great Mysterious," God who is untamed and too large to fit inside our neat and tidy boxes.

Rediscover Amazement

Nothing makes a roomful of people come alive like the presence of an infant. It is as though the baby gives them permission to be silly again, to rediscover for themselves what it is to be childlike again, to be amazed at the world as an infant is amazed. It is as though we can enter into that time that was once ours, when each moment was fresh and new. We can be ourselves, we can let the light and happy side of us come forth, and we are able to be energized afresh by God.

As the sensitive, God-filled poet Gerard Manley Hopkins tells us:

> The world is charged with grandeur of God.
>   It will flame out, like shining from shook foil;
>   It gathers to a greatness, like the ooze of oil
>
>   . . . .
>
> Because the Holy Ghost over the bent
>   World broods with warm breast and with ah!
>   bright wings.[1]

We too can see the glory by taking time to see what is in front of us, taking time to yearn and wait for Christ to come into the stuff of our everyday living.

I experienced one such encounter with wonder when I was in college; it shined out from the "shook foil" and sent me on an entirely new trajectory.

As a young boy, my encounters with God were rooted in the Baptist churches and my Native heritage, which I received from my "unisi," my beloved grandfather, Pop. Then, as a teen, I started attending a Presbyterian church, and I went on to study to become a Presbyterian minister at Belhaven University in Jackson, Mississippi.

Finding God in New Places

I had felt God's love both as a child and as a young man. Now I was trying to find God in books and study. I was living in my head, not in my heart. Day after day, I pored over dense philosophical books and scholarly scripture-study tomes. I read far more than was required, searching hard for something to touch my soul. I read daily about the love of God from masterful theologians like Karl Barth and Dietrich Bonhoeffer. My head was crammed full of knowledge but, at least at that time, my heart felt empty. I journeyed for a while through a wasteland. My inner landscape was as dry as the desert. I yearned for something more.

Then something happened that was to change my life forever. After spending spring break with my parents in Georgia, I passed through Selma, Alabama, where one of my high school teachers, who had remained a friend and mentor, had grown up. She invited me to visit a beautiful Catholic church there, and as I passed through town, I decided I would stop and do just that. I was curious, for I had never before set foot in a Catholic church, and I wondered what it would be like.

To my surprise, when I stepped inside the empty church, it looked very much like a Presbyterian church. The difference, however, is what mattered: up front was a gold box. I didn't know what it was, but I felt drawn toward it. It was as though God whispered in my ear saying, "Come closer."

I sat down in a pew directly in front of that box. At that moment, love flooded my heart; tenderness, melting compassion, and comfort rose up within me. Warmth coursed through my body. A quiet came over me that was nothing less than the peace of God. Time ceased to exist. This love was no theological abstraction. Rather, it was a great stream pouring through me from God's inmost being—a love that knows no pause. A memory was born that I would relish and draw upon for the rest of my life.

That moment sent me on a five-year journey that would end with my becoming Catholic. Even though I did not know what a tabernacle was, much less the Blessed Sacrament, Christ reached out of the tabernacle and kissed my heart with his love. Later I learned that the gold box was a tabernacle that contained the mystery and miracle of the Blessed Sacrament. Without knowing it, I was caught up in a powerful experience of Eucharistic Adoration; though I did not know with my head that the Blessed Sacrament was present—or what it was—I still felt the presence of Jesus there.

After that experience I grew more tenderhearted. It was easier to love others and be sensitive to their needs and feelings. From that moment, I had a much greater reservoir of compassion; I had experienced God's loving-kindness, and it helped me to empathize with those around me. What had started as a personal experience of God became one that included relationships with others.

Where Do You Find Wonder?

We live in a society that, for the most part, is absent of wonder. This society has lost its sense of mystery and, along with that, much joy. Ours is an age of anxiety, a secular age marked by narcissism and joylessness. Even within the Church, people are too often jaded and cynical, relating to one another through sterile electronics rather than in a face-to-face, eye-to-eye, human way that can pour joy over the encounter.

In his book *Recapturing the Wonder,* Mike Cosper describes our current predicament this way: "It's not a world entirely without God or a world without religion. Rather, it's a world where God and religion are superfluous. You can believe whatever you want so long as you don't expect it to affect your everyday experience."[2]

Most of us secretly yearn for a world that is not so antiseptic, a world soaked in the brightness of God. Western society once understood this intuitively; for at least a millennium and a half, the world was enchanted by God and God's creation. In the introduction to *The Book of Miracles,* Kenneth L. Woodward quotes St. Augustine, saying, "God himself has created all that is wonderful in this world, the great miracles as well as the minor marvels I have mentioned, and he has included them in all that unique wonder, the miracle of miracles, the world itself."[3]

Is there room for pleasure and fun in the joyful wonder Christ can bring? Christ's very first miracle in the Gospel of John was to change jugs of water into jugs of premium wine, to take what is part of human fun and infuse it with awe. In changing water into wine at the wedding banquet in Cana, Jesus showed himself to be a heightener of earthly joys and fun. He demonstrated his willingness to pour everlasting and pure joy into weary, thirsty hearts. He made the fun and pleasure of a party a wonder. That day, he made the joining of man and woman into a holy amazement.

The only true pathway into wonder is centering our whole being on God. It is as we meet God in the prayer of the silences, let him astonish us in the sacraments, and allow him to whisper into our hearts through scripture that we can see the world through the lenses of wonder. Real prayer does not so much make us otherworldly as give us the ability to see the world as enchanted by the mystery of God. The commonest joys are capable of this transformation. If we bring them to

Jesus, he will magnify them in the same way a taper plunged into a jar of oxygen blazes more brightly.

Lord of Wonder

Without Christ's presence, the brightest of earthly joys are like a stunning landscape in the evening shadow, which cannot be clearly seen. When the Lord comes to hallow them—as he always does when he is invited—the same scene bursts with new life; the sun blazes out on it, sparkling upon every bend of the undulating river, bringing beauty into shady corners and opening the flowers.

This smiling presence does not transform only our joys. It is true, the sunshine of his smile falls upon the water of human joy, transforming it into the wine of gladness. Yet he can also drop an elixir into the cups of sorrow and change them into cups of blessing and salvation. One drop of that potent influence can sweeten even bitter-tasting tears of pain. And the gifts he gives do not perish with the using. The more we take, the more we have. The largest water jugs will run dry at last; but Christ will give us a fountain within us springing unto life eternal.

In Jesus' closing words to the disciples before his passion in the Gospel of John, he claims to be in an altogether exceptional manner the object of the Father's love and—no less wonderful—to be able to love like the Father. "As the Father has loved me, so I have loved you; abide in my love. I have said these things to you so that my joy may be in you, and that your joy may be complete" (Jn 15:9, 11, NRSV:CE).

This was a strange time for Jesus to speak of his joy, with Gethsemane and Calvary so near. Was the Man of Sorrows a joyful man? Yes, Jesus had joy because he absolutely surrendered himself to the Father's will. This is the same joy he will give us if we too give up ourselves at the behest of love. Such joy will be progressive, ever full, and allow us to see the world with amazed eyes.

Pause in Wonder: A Moment with God

SCRIPTURE
As the Father loves me, so I also love you. Remain in my love. If you keep my commandments, you will remain in my love, just as I have kept my Father's commandments and remain in his love. I have told you this so that my joy may be in you and your joy may be complete (Jn 15:9–11).

PRAYER
Dear Lord, you live in majesty beyond all telling. Help me to stand on tiptoe with awe and wonder at your presence in our midst. You are the very bread and breath of life itself. Rekindle my heart when I am burned out, and gradually transform my sorrows into joy. I want to drink deeply from the living waters of your Spirit. Brighten the stuff of my daily living with your presence. Amen.

REFLECTION
The greatest gladness we will ever have is God. Like the infant John the Baptist leaping with joy in the womb, God wants to pass on to each of us, regardless of our age, the delight of being a child of an all-loving Father. We wait on tiptoe for Christ's coming glory. After hostility, there will be forgiveness; after estrangement, reconciliation; after oppression and dehumanization, justice; after death, homecoming and resurrection.

Starters for Journaling or Meditation

- What are some of the "awe triggers" in your life? Perhaps hearing a stirring liturgy or a great hymn, watching the soft breathing of a newborn, or a walking in nature brings you to awe. Slow down and take time to notice these triggers, then write them down.

- Has there been a time in your life when you have seen sorrow become joy? Describe it.

- Draw a simple sketch or picture with pen or pencil to describe a time in your life you stood in awe of God's world and were touched by joy.

Two

JOY IS A CHOICE

Joy is the settled assurance that God is in control of all the details of my life, the quiet confidence that ultimately everything is going to be all right, and the determined choice to praise God in all things.
—KAY WARREN, *CHOOSE JOY*

Pop used to repeat an old Native story, that we all have two dogs inside us, fighting for dominance: One is vengeful, bitter, resentful, and hateful, always striking out. The other is calm, peaceful, and abounding with joy.

"Which dog wins?" I asked him.

He replied, "The one you feed."

Which dog are you feeding?

We can feed resentment and bitterness, or we can feed the part of us that is loving and sensitive to God and his world. The choice is up to us.

We can feed what is good in us through prayer, meditation, spiritual reading, and acts of kindness. Of course, we will also experience feelings of negativity, anger, and revenge, but we need not entertain them. We can simply be aware that they are there, and take them to a loving God who can drown the bitterness in a sea of love. In doing this, with God's help we become custodians of our thoughts and emotions. We

can ask the Holy Spirit to fill us with life-giving thoughts and
emotions, and continually choose joy.

How Can I Choose Joy?

Here are some practical ways you can begin to choose joy.

Resist discontentment. One step in choosing joy is to look
at the rumblings, the thoughts and the images of our heart.
Whatever we concentrate on becomes the inclination of our
lives. Each time we entertain feelings of discontentment, comparing ourselves unfavorably against those who are well-off
financially, have a prestigious job, or have a perfect spouse and
family, we are condemned to an unhappy, joyless life.

It is so easy to blame others for our unhappiness and to
hold on to spiteful thoughts. Our stomachs twist with worry
over seen and unseen perils lurking just around the corner.
Whatever we ponder, we can become.

Cherish beauty. I once heard it said that the human brain is
like Velcro when it comes to bad experiences but like Teflon
when it comes to the positive, peaceful part of reality. The
reality of biblical faith is that through God's grace we can
choose to some extent what to think about. With the help
of his Spirit, we can become like Velcro to peaceful joy. We
can take special times each day to concentrate on our blessed
memories, our joyful times, the times of wonder when God
blasted us with light and sound like a firecracker. Paul states
this eloquently in Philippians:

> Finally, beloved, whatever is true, whatever is hon-
> orable, whatever is just, whatever is pure, whatever
> is pleasing, whatever is commendable, if there is
> any excellence and if there is anything worthy of
> praise, think about these things. Keep on doing

> the things that you have learned and received and
> heard and seen in me, and the God of peace will
> be with you. (Phil 4:8, NRSV:CE)

As this scripture points out, one of the primary ways our
hearts are fashioned for wonder is to cherish everything that
is beautiful, all that is lovely. Any radiant gift dropped suddenly into our lives, any water of gladness sprinkled along
our path, is due to him—a beam from the Father of Light,
the glint of his smile.

Therefore, let us turn away from the things that upset
and exasperate us in the circumstances and persons around
us. Instead we can focus on the traits that are delightful and
attractive. Dwell on these. Count that in everything and everyone there is something that God can love. Look for God, and
thank him for all the ways he shows himself in your life. And
thus, the beautiful, true, and good will be a sparkling ladder
to climb into the wonderment of his presence.

Take time to ponder. In many ways our lives are like the Rosary; we have sorrowful mysteries, but we also have joyful mysteries. The fact you are reading this book suggests that at some
time in your life you wanted God to touch you, and you now
hope to experience his closeness.

Take a moment to ponder some of those times from your
past. Perhaps it was at your First Communion, the first time the
Bible came alive for you, at your wedding or the birth of a child,
or a time you were driving in nature and you came across a
scene so stunning, you said to yourself, "There must be a God."
It is as though each of us has a treasure chest in our hearts that
contains precious, gleaming jewelry. When we stop and look at
that jewelry, the joy-making power of those treasures, the graces
of the past burst out into the present, and delight can flood us.

In the Hebrew and Christian traditions, remembering is a form of prayer. Part of our prayer each day can be taking time to actively recollect. In doing so, we imitate our Blessed Mother. Scripture tells us, "And Mary kept all these things, reflecting on them in her heart" (Lk 2:19).

Remembering My Boyhood Legacy

I learned that memory can be a powerful religious experience by spending time in my grandparents' little stucco cabin on a bluff high above the whitewater rapids of the Chattahoochee River.

My paternal great-grandmother, Mary Alexander Ensley, was a full-blooded Cherokee. She lived in the mountains of North Carolina where she reared her children, including my grandfather whom I called "Pop." Though she died a little before my birth, I knew her well through Pop and my father. Her bronze skin tone and angular face set her apart in the white Southern culture. When she was a child, her family was burned out of their farm because they were different. In the part of Georgia where she settled later in her life, she was often shunned. Despite all she suffered, she was a healer who could help cure infection with molds and herbs. She could quiet hearts with a song or chant. She delivered scores of babies.

She was tough, too. Daddy said she carried a small pistol in her apron, determined she would not be burned out again, and supplemented the family income through operating a still back in the deep woods. Sometimes I think Daddy was embellishing when he told me about the still because I never heard a word about it from my grandfather and Daddy's eyes twinkled when he told me. Nevertheless, my great-grandmother was a strong yet tender healer who held on to her Native tradition for dear life. She made sure she passed it on to Pop and Daddy, who then passed it on to me.

Pop sang me some of the old chants when I was little. They conveyed great joy as they soothed my heart; the rhythm of them cleansed my soul. Like his mother, Pop was a Baptist Christian. The two of them saw no conflict between holding on to cherished elements of their Native culture and holding on to Jesus and the Bible.

Embracing the Hard Places

It was through Pop that I learned what it is to be Indian. Pop and his wife, "Granny," who also had some Native blood, became a joyful oasis in the often gloomy and troubled time of my early childhood. Both my parents loved me dearly, but not always well. I was a footling breech birth with umbilical cord strangulation. I was blue from lack of oxygen, and the obstetrician said if it had been a few more seconds, I would have been born dead.

Because of this and other, possible gestational, issues, I was born with a neurocognitive brain impairment. I had a visual-spatial impairment with some motor difficulty. The part of my brain that handled words worked well, even early on. I later tested near-genius when it came to the ability to use words, but my nonverbal performance IQ testing dipped into the major impairment range.

This was all a puzzle to my parents, who did not understand why I was messy, clumsy, and awkward, and why I stumbled in tasks like tying my shoes or buttoning my shirts. The ordinary tasks of living presented a daily challenge. When I was little, my parents showered affection on me, letting me know I was wanted. But as I grew older, my parents, especially my mother, thought that the way to cure me was to shame me.

When I was five, tragedy struck. My beloved father experienced a sudden onset of mental illness, a psychotic break.

The psychiatrist diagnosed him with paranoid schizophrenia. When he was in the throes of psychotic delusions, he became terrifying. I can still recall one incident when, his eyes beaming hatred, his voice quivering, he took me aside one evening and, using his finger to imitate a knife, crisscrossed my belly. He told me, "If you misbehave, I will cut you open from here to here."

Over time, God gave me courage to remember and face the pain of those times, summoning them up from where for so long I had hidden and repressed them, and inviting God in to heal that old pain. The Jewish people, when God led them on their mighty deliverance in the Exodus, had to first acknowledge the harshness of their former captivity before they could experience the utter joy of their liberation. And so it is for all of us.

When I think of those hard times, there are bright spots, too—particularly memories of my grandparents, who were my only relief other than my nightly prayer times. They both loved God intensely, and they were my solace, my stronghold, and my fortress. At their house, in their presence, I was safe, able to experience joy and laughter.

A big, white Bible sat on the coffee table, and Granny, who had learned to read through an adult literacy program, often sounded out the words for us. As she read, a deep stillness settled on the three of us. Those words medicated my young and troubled soul, dissolving for a while my fears and terror.

Recalling God's Goodness

Much of what Granny and Pop did in that house was remember. Together they vividly recalled and relived the ways God had brightened their lives; together we remembered the people who had animated their lives, and we cherished the joys of their Native culture. Everything stopped when a certain song came in over the radio. The song, which was really their anthem, was "Precious Memories." When it played, Granny stopped whatever she was doing, sometimes leaning on her broom as the song played, tears trickling down her face. Pop would tear up, too, as they both mouthed the words:

> Precious mem'ries, how they linger,
> How they ever flood my soul;
> In the stillness of the midnight,
> Precious, sacred scenes unfold.[1]

I used to pepper Pop with questions about the old days. He told me how, in the times before his birth, canoes called dugouts could be built from trees hollowed out with hot embers and axes. He shared how arrowheads were flacked and shaped from stone. He also told about the terrible times when the soldiers imprisoned our ancestors, confiscating their farms and houses, locking our people in open stockades that we would call concentration camps today. Many thousands were sent on a death march to the West called the Trail of Tears.

Despite all that pain, he told me of many joyful times growing up, including fishing in the French Broad River. He recounted playful, wondrous stories of our people: about the diminutive Cherokee angels, called *nunnehi* (the immortals), whose help and influence was mighty as they served the Lord and his people. Their ears would perk up if you spoke Cherokee to them. He claimed some lived in the woods below his house.

I know Pop spent lots of time, silent with eyes closed, in his easy chair remembering happy times. He rested in the stillness, letting the stillness infuse his heart with God.

I didn't know it at the time, but Pop was teaching me to be a contemplative. He didn't know this, either—Pop had never heard the words "contemplative prayer," but that was what he was doing. His rich silences taught me to be comfortable with the stillness. He could tell when I was caught up in pain and fear from my parents' home, and he would help me redirect my thoughts by taking me up to the edge of the bluff as we looked at the lovely scene below.

I remember the first time my father was hospitalized for mental illness. He started mumbling gibberish at work, and the nurse at the factory immediately took him to the mental ward at the local hospital. They wanted my mother to be at his side as he went through various treatments, including electro-shock and insulin shock therapy. My mother sent me to my grandparents, who looked after me. I did not understand what was going on; it felt as though my parents were abandoning me. And yet my grandparents carried me through with lots of love, happy stories, and God.

At this point I also feel that I need to make a special comment about my parents, as throughout this book I make reference to dysfunctional family dynamics and the verbal, emotional, and physical abuse that were part of my early life. Both my parents were struggling with their own illnesses and issues, and yet, despite all these things, my parents genuinely and profoundly loved me. We still had beautiful moments even in the midst of the dysfunction.

When I was fourteen my father's delusions stopped and his psychiatric illness went into near permanent remission. When I was a young adult, my mother quit drinking and slowly recovered. As my parents rediscovered each other and their love for each other blossomed, my father took the role of healer and mentor in my life. In their retirement they both were so proud of me and showed it in numerous ways. My dad helped me own and recover my Native heritage and was a great source of nurture and comfort for me, becoming the wonderful kind of father any young man would wish for. In their retirement we took many joyful trips and vacations that were both fun and grace filled. In their later years, my parents discovered the Catholic Church on their own and became Catholic. I am so grateful for them both—and for my grandparents, who were always there for me in those intervening years.

Take Time to Reverence God in Nature

The first morning I was staying with my grandparents, Pop woke me up and said, "Let's go for a walk." Every morning he engaged in a ritual Cherokees call "going to water." Originally that meant immersing yourself in a running stream. For Pop, at his age, it meant looking at and reverencing the Chattahoochee below his home.

This particular morning he said a prayer he had said at other times to greet Grandmother Sun. It was obviously a prayer that had been handed on to him. He recited each line and paused afterward for me to repeat after him. We prayed:

> Good morning, Grandmother Sun
> I stand in the midst of your sunrays
> I stand in the midst of your sunrays
> And by the Creator I am blessed.

As I participated in this ritual with him, I was lost for a while in the joy of wonderment. Later, as a Catholic, I discovered that Native American Christians can hold on to Christ even as they cherish elements of their sacred traditions that do not contradict the faith.

One of the beautiful things I found in Catholicism was that the Church believes in the kind of enculturation that redeems and purifies not just individuals but the whole created order. "Cultures must also be purified and restored in Christ."[2] Throughout history, the Church has spread the message of God's love using the symbols of particular cultures. This is especially a good thing for me as a Native American.

In 1987, Pope St. John Paul II met with ten thousand Native Americans in Phoenix, Arizona. A Native medicine man and third-generation Catholic led the pope through a blessing ceremony. He also went through several Native American healing ceremonies. John Paul II encouraged Native Americans to keep the cultural ways as long as they were in accord with Christ. This greatly encouraged me to include my culture in my spiritual journey, the culture I learned from my father and my grandfather who were both Native American and baptized Christians.

We choose joy by feeding our souls with the brightness of life. No matter how dire our circumstances, we all have had our own precious memories. All too often that treasure trove of memory is under lock and key. Often that part of us is under siege. Just as we take time to contemplate our worries, we can take time to contemplate our joys. When we do, the delight of those times can astonish us again even as new wonder erupts in our souls.

Pause in Wonder: A Moment with God

SCRIPTURE

May you be made strong with all the strength that comes from his glorious power, and may you be prepared to endure everything with patience, while joyfully giving thanks to the Father, who has enabled you to share in the inheritance of the saints in the light. He has rescued us from the power of darkness and transferred us into the kingdom of his beloved

Son, in whom we have redemption, the forgiveness of sins.
(Col 1:11–14, NRSV:CE)

Prayer
Dear Lord, thank you for the newness, the freshness, the vigor
that is your joy. Help me not to ignore my troubles or deny
them but in the midst of them choose you and your joy. Guide
me in remembering the joyful mysteries of my life. Help me
see clearly the bright threads that are sewed into the fabric of
my love, for you are the God who resides in the majesty of
delight and joy. Help me to remember you, think of you, and
widen my heart to receive your splendor. Amen.

Reflection
I was speaking at a meeting in Mexico City. In my free time
I thought it would be inspiring to see the sacred cloth that
contained the image of Mary as Our Lady of Guadalupe,
which portrays Mary as a Native woman. It ended up being a
pilgrimage that infused my life with amazing joy. I saw tens
of thousands of people, many who were Native, many with
tattered clothes that indicated their poverty, praying in the
huge square that led to the basilica. Most of them were on
their knees inching forward, saying and chanting prayers as
tears rolled down their faces. Powerful waves of wonderment
swept through all of us. These people, despite their poverty,
chose the joy of this wondrous place, not just in their minds
but in their hearts and their entire bodies. Never have I seen
such a depth of belief in one place.

Today, like the crowd and like Juan Diego who first saw
the Lady, we are called to believe that, whatever our state in
life, we can choose joy. The holy simplicity of heart of the
people at the shrine taught me that faith moves not toward
complexity but toward simplicity. God is with you today, just

as surely as he is with the people at the shrine. Take some time today and choose to bask in his presence and let his nearness gladden your heart.

Christ is coming, and we can make straight the pathways for him in our hearts every day. Examine your soul each day. Are there resentments inside you? Take time to tell him about those resentments and let his presence take away their sting. When possible, reconcile with others. Clearing our lives of the clutter that comes from disharmony with others will smooth the pathway to God being born afresh in our hearts. When we make interior and exterior paths for God, he can lift up and re-create the neglected, lowly, outcast parts of ourselves.

Starters for Journaling or Meditation

- Think of some of the times you consciously turned away from self-absorption, even self-pity, to a bright reality. Meditate or write about those moments. How did remembering such times change how you felt?

- Like the Rosary, we each have our sorrowful mysteries as well as our joyful and glorious mysteries. We need to deal with the sorrowful mysteries. Yet we should take time for the wondrous joyful mysteries that are also part of our lives. Think of a few such mysteries in your own life.

Three

FINDING JOY IN SACRAMENTALITY

Thou art like silence unperplexed,
*   A secret and a mystery*
Between one footfall and the next.
    —Alice Meynell, "To the Beloved"[1]

It was not a time when I would have expected to experience joy. Two of my friends, Dan Almeter and Chuck Hornsby, had driven across the state from the Alleluia Community, a covenant community where I am a mission member, to visit me. I had just finished telling them about the darkest scenes from my trauma-filled childhood. My chest tight and throat squeezing, I had shared those scenes of pain with my friends. I had spoken about these moments with counselors in the past and had even written about some of those scenes in my books. However, I had never told them all at one time, and this time I shared some of my more tightly guarded secrets, which I had never told anyone before.

As I mentioned earlier, my father suffered from a delusional mental illness that could terrify me at times. My mother was often harried by the terror she faced from Daddy. She had no adult to turn to, so she turned to me. I remember a time when I was five, and Daddy was terrorizing us. She sat me on her lap, caressing my hair and saying with a laser-focused gaze, "Your father doesn't love me; nobody has ever loved me except you, Eddie. You are the first person who has ever loved me."

Another time she said to me, desperately holding on to me, smothering me with her affection, "When you grow up and fall in love and get married, you and I will have a secret: You will love me more than your wife." I remember feeling special and connected with my mother, but even more than that I was drowning in an overpowering sea of emotions that burdened me with responsibility no little boy should bear. Her happiness and well-being were in my hands. No five-year-old should be forced to bear the weight of that.

As I recounted these stories to Chuck and Dan, I felt that not only were they listening to me, but God was also listening to me. I asked them to pray for me. It was the first time I had asked for prayer for all these issues at once.

Dan lightly sprinkled me with holy water. That water unleashed a sea of joy in my heart. Tension began leaving my body. I felt the drops of gladness not only touch my skin but well up inside me, cleansing me, standing me on tiptoe with joy. I thought of the pure water of baptism, the living water Jesus described to the woman at the well, the kind of water that wells up into eternal life.

Chuck gently placed and held a crucifix to my cheeks. My own personal torture was knit together with Jesus' torture and death, with his suffering and resurrection. Whereas minutes before, I had felt the shame of some of my history, now I felt connected with Jesus in the bosom of my soul. I felt that Jesus was truly my brother and that his Father was my father, too. His love emptied me of all concerns and worries. Jesus looked down on me with love, and I felt my heart reflected in his tender gaze.

It was a powerful experience of sacramentality. The sacramentals of the water and the crucifix engaged my senses and reminded me of the healing mystery that surrounds our lives, conveying the depth of God in tangible ways.

What Is the Sacramental Life?

Long before I ever set foot in a Catholic church, I experienced the power of sacramentality, the sights, sounds, tastes, and smells of human life on this earth that put me in touch with God.

My Cherokee grandfather, Pop, never heard the word *sacrament*, but the rituals and habits of this sensory world tied him to the Creator and the Creator's world. Each morning he took the long, steep track to the river to honor the water. Sometimes he took me with him; there was a special spot between the power station and steep slope to the river. He would greet Grandmother Sun, and there was an interchange of stillness between Pop's heart and the water below and the rising sun. He would sometimes chant and sing there, his eyes going up, looking heavenward. He told me once, his voice taking on a wistful tone, that this was what he called the remembering spot, a place I could return to all my life and remember him and all he had taught me.

This remembering spot made a profound impression on me as a boy. It was as if Pop were drawing on a deep quiet from creation, a quiet in which God came to us, showing his tender love through the things he made. Pop's gourd shaker raised the sound of wordless prayer up to heaven. Together in the house, he and Granny read from the Bible with a reverence that reminded me of the Liturgy of the Word, which

I came to later understand and appreciate in an even deeper way as a Catholic.

Though as a boy I had no understanding of blessings, Pop blessed me often. His tobacco pipe was always handy. It was not a ritual or peace pipe, just a regular wood pipe. If I were particularly troubled, he would have me sit on the ottoman facing his big easy chair. It was my favorite place in the house.

Pop and I would face each other, and he would blow smoke all around me till it encircled me, calming me, settling me down, inducting me into the presence of the Holy. I later came to understand that he was blessing me with the smoke, using it as a catalyst of prayer. I would often think of this each time I saw a priest or deacon bless the altar and the congregation with incense.

Within the Catholic Church parents and grandparents have the authority to bless their children (*CCC*, 2228). Though Pop was not a Catholic, this was what he was doing, and it bore much fruit in my life.

God cannot be wrapped up in one idea, one concept, one way of working in the lives of human beings. We may say many wonderful things about God. We describe God as being, beauty, love, and good. All those positive things about God are true as far as they go. However, we cannot grasp the infinite and uncreated God, even with inspiring concepts. God is always more, always beyond. God is mystery, always greater, more beautiful, more alive than we dare expect. We can experience this infinite more only as mystery. Native people are dead-on when they call the Creator the Great Mysterious.

Yet, Christians believe that things we experience through our senses like incense, water, bells, and the whole of our earthly existence hold the potential of ushering us into the embrace of God. As limited, finite human beings we can only experience the unbounded God through our earthliness, our humanity. Human experiences such as consolation during loss of a loved one, a baby being born, a time when true beauty intrudes, can cause our hearts to dance that God is so near. Human experiences have the possibility to brighten and lift up our being with the sacred in meeting God, so close we can all but touch him. This is what it means to live a truly sacramental life.

When we attune our hearts to finding God in creation, we find that he extends himself to us again and again, often in unexpected ways. Such experiences point beyond themselves to God. Just as a novel points us to the novelist's mind and a painting points beyond itself to the heart of the artist, so all creation can point to the Creator and help us taste of the Creator's ecstatic delight in this world he has made.

Rituals, sacred music, and liturgy can take our hearts and sweep us up into an immense joy. We kneel, bow, and make the Sign of the Cross. With our bodies we make gestures. All this is sacramental. The significant seven ceremonies for Catholics are called sacraments; they guarantee a direct encounter with God.

Finding Jesus in the Sacraments

Sacraments are mystery-filled, concrete signs and touchpoints that enable us to experience and be captivated by infinite joy, love, and beauty. We experience water flowing over us, smell the fragrant sacred oil sliding across our foreheads, feel the roundness of wedding bands on our fingers, or experience the stole tying us hand and heart to the bishop in ordination.

Jesus, the center of Christian faith, is the sacrament of sacraments, for in him God comes to us as human. We taste him, touch him, and consume him physically in the Eucharist, and all seven sacraments disclose him. The summit of the sacraments is the celebration of the Eucharist, in which we physically contact and partake in this unspeakable mystery of beauty and love as we invite the loving and beautiful One to enter our very bodies. It is a glimpse of heaven on earth.

As Pope Benedict XVI states, "It is not the Eucharistic food that is changed into us, but rather we who are mysteriously transformed by it. Christ nourishes us by uniting us to himself; 'he draws us into himself.'"[2] Bread is the staff of life, but blood is the life. So "this cup" teaches that the life of Jesus Christ must pass into his people's veins, and that the secret of the Christian life is "yet I live, no longer I, but Christ lives in me" (Gal 2:20). The Christian life is not only to be a feeding on Christ as its nourishment, but a glad partaking, as at a feast, of his life and thereby of his joy. The Eucharist is the capstone of the other six sacraments and all sacramentals.

Earlier in this book, I described a powerful experience I had as a young man, stepping into a Catholic church and encountering Jesus in the tabernacle for the first time (see page 4). After I had this special meeting with God, I yearned for more. I yearned to actually attend one of those Catholic services, the Mass. I chose St. Richard of Chichester Church in Jackson, Mississippi. The celebrant was the pastor, Monsignor Josiah Chatham. He was partially paralyzed from multiple sclerosis and said Mass from a walker.

Despite his disability, his facial muscles, his body stance, and his voice communicated vast joy. His face took on a beatific look as he said the words of consecration. In a way I can't fully explain, it seemed as if heaven was touching earth. The past, future, and present met in one timeless moment. I could feel my eyes well up. I knew where the monsignor's joy came from; it came from the Eucharist. That same joy stopped

time for me as I sat there, absorbed in wonder. I knew my life
could never be the same.

The Gift of Sacred Imagination

Through the sacraments, we have the opportunity to encounter God and grow in relationship with him. The sacraments
engage our imagination in a unique way. As theologians
from St. Augustine to St. Bonaventure were quick to point
out, sight is our primary means of cognition, and the imagination is central to the process of conversion. Theologian
Kathleen Fischer states, "The imagination enables us to live
in multi-leveled, multi-colored truth, and to receive the truth
which is pervaded by mist and mystery."[3]

Avery Dulles, S.J., writes that revelation "is mediated
through symbol—that is to say, through an externally per-
ceived sign that works mysteriously on the human consciousness so as to suggest more than it can clearly describe
or define."[4] When we perceive the full significance of these
signs, the sacraments become for us conveyors of infinite joy.
The sacraments burst into us, body and soul, to remake us
and delight us.

There is no better way to understand the main Gospel
truths than through imagery and our senses. Metaphor, poetry, nonverbal signs, and symbols enliven the part of the brain
built for sacred experience, but metaphor does not point to
more metaphor, nor does religious poetic language point to
more poetry. That which gives religious poetry and metaphor
its meaning is real in an absolute, ultimate, and unconditioned
way. Genuine religious imagination always points to something ultimate.

When we allow ourselves to engage our God-given imagi-
nations, asking God to reveal to us what he wants us to see, we

open our hearts wide to joy. Sacramentals like holy water, the Rosary, the Stations of the Cross, though not full sacraments, can express what is called sacramentality: concrete signs of God. They stimulate our ability to imagine, which is why they contain so much power to change us.

Drama, art, even the miracle of creation itself, if we allow it, can mesmerize with the core realities of faith. A simple loaf of bread can remind us of the Eucharist, pouring water can remind us of baptism, and blowing wind can remind of the breath of the Spirit.

Pause in Wonder: A Moment with God

SCRIPTURE

While they were eating, Jesus took a loaf of bread, and after blessing it he broke it, gave it to the disciples, and said, "Take, eat; this is my body." Then he took a cup, and after giving thanks he gave it to them, saying, "Drink from it, all of you; for this is my blood of the covenant, which is poured out for many for the forgiveness of sins. I tell you, I will never again drink of this fruit of the vine until that day when I drink it new with you in my Father's kingdom." (Mt 26:26–29, NRSV:CE)

PRAYER

Dear Lord, you meet us in nature, in sunlight and sunset, in mountain and in field. You refresh us with water and feed us with bread made from swaying grain; you lighten our hearts with wine made from a field of grapes. Nature and the stuff of creation that meets our senses can all point to a God of unfathomable love. In the sacraments, nature, bread and wine, oil and water, you become touchable. Open me up daily to all the signs of your presence. Amen.

REFLECTION

It is often remarked that the Gospel is expressed in the preached Word, but the Gospel is shown in the sacraments. The God of the scriptures prefers sensory language and sensory experience to appeal to us sensory creatures.

The sacraments use imaginative language to express the immaterial in ways that can charm us with the realities behind the mysteries enacted. The acting out of Gospel realities in the sacraments conveys a depth that cannot be expressed in abstract propositions. Connecting with God in sacramental ways can gladden us beyond measure.

Starters for Journaling or Meditation

- In the Eucharist, bread and wine, God becomes touchable, a part of our very being. Write about a time the Eucharist brightened your life with joy.

- Where else do you experience the sacramental life—what rituals or tangible reminders of God help you to ponder the great mysteries?

- Recall a time you had a heartfelt experience of the nearness of God. Remember that time vividly and let the grace of that time erupt in your everyday life. Write about what you experience.

Four

FINDING JOY IN ETERNITY

O gentle hand! O delicate touch, which has the taste of eternal life!
—St. John of the Cross

I was not usually a naturally joyous or happy person growing up; we didn't have much laughter, happiness, or joy in my parents' home. My solace was to have a wonderful extended family of grandparents and aunts and uncles and cousins. My Aunt Lovey, my dad's sister, was a buoyant woman with an uncontainable smile who introduced me to fun, laughter, and joy.

As with Pop, God showed on her face. I felt safe and whole when I was around her. She took me to the fascinating lights of the fair, school carnivals, movies, and the rodeo with my cousin Ernest, her grandson. She told us jokes so funny that we would belly laugh. Because of her, some happiness and joy touched my life.

One morning when I was nine years old, I had a vivid dream of loud church bells ringing that woke me up: it was the telephone ringing. My sleepy mother finally answered—then

shrieked loudly and collapsed into sobs. It was Lovey's daughter, Margie. Aunt Lovey was dead, killed in a car accident a
hundred miles away near Troy, Alabama.

My insides quivered as I heard those words.

Margie joined us, and we all piled into the car. Daddy
immediately started driving Margie, Ernest, Mother, and me
to the hospital to pick up Lovey's shaken but uninjured husband, who had wrecked the car.

The accident had wrecked my world as well. A kaleido-
scope of terror and pain washed over me; my stomach was
fluttery and nauseated. It was the first time I faced death
up close, and I struggled to grapple with the reality that my
beloved aunt was gone. There would be no more laughter, trips
to the carnival, or drive-in movies.

I saw her in the casket, and it seemed as if tight ropes
squeezed around my insides. The funeral was at a Baptist
church. My parents had not attended church in a long time
but, because of my grandparents, the Baptist faith had become
a safe place for me. Even at an early age, I had loved the reading of scripture and the words of the pastor. As the funeral
unfolded, the pastor read comforting scripture in a way that
washed over my terrified soul.

Even now, I remember the lyrical soothing words of the
King James Version: "Come unto me, all ye that labour and
are heavy laden, and I will give you rest" (Mt 11:28), and, "Let
not your heart be troubled: ye believe in God, believe also in
me. In my Father's house are many mansions: if it were not so,
I would have told you. I go to prepare a place for you. And if I
go and prepare a place for you, I will come again, and receive
you unto myself; that where I am, ye may be also" (Jn 14:1–3).

These scriptures settled down my inner being, touching
me with a bottomless stillness that comforted my anxious

soul. As I continued to ponder the words about the realities of heaven, wells of profound and calming joy swept through me. The scriptures knitted my soul with the deep mystery of God behind the words. I had fallen in love with the words of Jesus.

After the funeral, I began reading a New Testament that had the words of Jesus printed in red. As I read those words, in spite of the terrible times that came later, in unexpected times and ways that cannot be explained, joy touched my soul. I was learning the first lesson about joy: Great consolation can come in the midst of tragedy. Death doesn't have the final word. Because of Jesus, we have an eternal, soul-lifting hope.

Rejoice in the Hope of Heaven?

At Aunt Lovey's funeral, the scriptures on eternal life brought me wonder and joy mixed in with a profound sense of loss. Meditating on eternal life through reading the scriptures (even when we are not grieving or near death) can infuse our world with a touch of glory, imbuing us with a hope that lasts forever.

St. Faustina describes an experience of heaven in regular life:

> Today I was in heaven, in spirit, and I saw its inconceivable beauties and the happiness that awaits us after death. . . . I saw how great is happiness in God, which spreads to all creatures, making them happy; and then all the glory and praise which springs from this happiness returns to its source; and they enter into the depths of God, contemplating the inner life of God, the Father, the Son, and the Holy Spirit, whom they will never comprehend or fathom. This source of happiness is unchanging in its essence, but it is always new, gushing forth happiness for all creatures.[1]

Our touches of eternity may not be as vivid as Faustina's, but we can still let heaven intrude. In the New Testament the reality of eternal reconciliation—when all will be made new again—is a powerful font of joy. Just knowing that each day, each second of every day, is pulled toward glory and the New Jerusalem can thrill our souls deep down. This is the hope of every Christian: that there will one day be no more sorrow, no more tears, for "He will wipe every tear from their eyes, and there shall be no more death or mourning, wailing or pain, [for] the old order has passed away" (Rv 21:4).

The Joy of the New Jerusalem

The experience of awe I felt as I listened to the scripture readings at Aunt Lovey's funeral is not unique to me—others in similar situations have reported a sense of being touched by God in their grief, allowing them to anticipate with joy the world to come, the new heaven and earth sometimes called the "New Jerusalem."

This sense of renewal and transformation—not just of ourselves, but of all creation—is something that is uniquely Christian. The resurrection of Jesus Christ altered the course of creation. If we take time to meditate on this reality, before long we will find ourselves standing on tiptoe with wonder. This can often be hard during bereavement and other times of loss, but by reading the scriptures of eternal life and acknowledging the pull of heaven, when we hardly expect it, consolation can come. We are like a sailboat. We can put out the sail of hope, but the boat remains stuck in the water till finally the wind of the Holy Spirit blows again, our sail fills up, and our boat speeds on its journey. The wind of hope, like the wind of faith, is a gift. We cannot manufacture hope, but we can put out the sail to catch the wind of the Spirit when the wind blows.

In some places in scripture, the very words that describe eternal life carry us into a transcendent state of intense gladness and well-being. For instance, here is another passage from Revelation, describing worship in the New Jerusalem. Read this passage slowly, and let it catapult your soul upward, and caress you with joy:

> They will not hunger or thirst anymore,
> nor will the sun or any heat strike them.
> For the Lamb who is in the center of the throne
>   will shepherd them
> and lead them to springs of life-giving water,
> and God will wipe away every tear from their eyes.
> (Rv 7:16–17)

Long before our Lord walked this world, carrying the keys of resurrection and life, people held some hope of eternal life. The Gospel simply threw fuller light on that which had been before partially hidden, as the rising sun reveals the clear outlines of the landscape that had lain indistinct and hazy in the gray dawn. Christ drew from the window the curtain through which the morning light had been feebly struggling to reach the sleeper's eyes.

"Catch Some of the Glory"

Pop was especially sensitive to spiritual realities, and he often reminded me that many angels are always around us. "Watch carefully when you go into the woods," he said to me. "Turn around and you may well encounter angels there dressed in deerskin that glows with the breath of Edota" ["the dearly beloved father" in Cherokee, another name for God]. "Stay there long enough and your heart will catch some of the glory."

I'm sure that Pop caught some of the glory from down in the woods. Looking back on this with eyes informed by the spiritual reality of the Church, I understand that being in the woods alone meant being in solitude. It is as we make that space in our hearts in solitude that we are most attentive to the spiritual.

It may be that one of the reasons Pop communed so readily with spiritual reality was an experience he had before my birth. Part of his duties in working for the cotton mill was climbing down steep brick stairs to check on a little pump house for the mill. One day he accidentally stepped onto a live electric cable. He was seriously injured and then, in a miracle of sorts, woke up to everyday reality. He said he died and imperishable glory shone around him. He said that the *gowheli* (leaves) emanated light, and even the *tibi* (buzzing bee) shone with glory. Everything was glorious, and all reality—the river, the rapids, the sun, the sky—was knit together in strands of light.

In his vision, he saw Jesus across the river, beckoning with outstretched arms. Jesus said, "You will have to wait awhile till you see me again; go back, and I entrust you with the care and teaching of all your children and grandchildren." What is significant is that the woods, the sky, the bees, the rock, and the water were all brought into harmony and utter newness by Jesus. In his Native eye, Pop saw the interconnectedness of all things in God. He recounted this experience to me many times.

The reality of eternity can interrupt and brighten our lives at different times. Eternity's touch can help soothe some of the hurting scenes with hope. Whenever we struggle with sadness, the reality of eternal life can nurture us with the touch of forever.

For instance, my neurological disability weighed me down and caused me shame, especially when I was in school. My disability made it very difficult, if not impossible, for me to play sports when I was young, but that didn't keep me from wanting to play. There was a group of us in the neighborhood that would play backyard sports. The other kids tolerated my awkwardness and clumsiness. I was always the last one picked, but I was always welcome. Even though I never scored and even though it was difficult, they were kind to me and never made fun of me. They were always there to be my friends, and I thoroughly enjoyed taking part in the games.

But when I tried out for Little League Baseball, it was a different story. I attempted several things in the tryouts but was clumsy and flubbed all the various positions I was supposed to play. I was rejected after failing to catch even one ball. I was deeply embarrassed in front of the coach and everyone else. Not being able to play sports, which I would have loved to have done, was a major source of shame for me. When I hit junior high, I made a mess of all things that required physical skill. I loved the world of art, including pictures and the art that I found in books. However, due to my disability, my own attempts at creating art with watercolors or pastels came out poorly. I always felt very inadequate.

Then, about a year ago, I had a dream. I was back in school. It's not clear whether it was high school or college or afterward, but there was a coach and a team, and I played perfectly. I was selected for all the different sports teams: basketball, baseball, and football. I could handle the ball with ease, movement came naturally to me, and I had no motor problems like I do in real life. The coach followed me around and encouraged me. Then he looked at me and said, "Eddie, you're a beautiful athlete." I felt an enormous grace that I knew to be the grace of God. This coach was enabling me to do things I had never done. In that dream I also hiked up a mountain and drew pictures that were beautiful. In the dream, I knew that my disability wasn't there anymore. My heart was full of love for others. I knew that the coach was the one who enabled me. Just by being in his presence, things were OK.

It was only upon awakening that the identity of the coach became clear to me: he was Jesus, not with the long beard and robes, but appearing like a coach in his late thirties. In that dream I saw God's presence saturating the earth, in the very ground beneath my feet. I saw many different people, and it was so easy to love them all.

I still do not fully understand the meaning of this dream. I believe it is telling me of a future glory—the new creation, the New Jerusalem—that we are moving toward rapidly. In that glory I will be able to experience all those things I wish I could have experienced while growing up, all the things that, even now, I still miss. The dream of the coach was followed by a series of dreams of being able to do things that are not in my capacity, like hiking up mountains and playing basketball. In those dreams and in the dream of the coach, God pulled me close, gladdening me. All that I saw was a mirror reflecting his image. I was experiencing a taste of glory, when all things will be made new and whole. I awakened, my eyes filled with happy tears and a deep appreciation of this everyday world and everything in it.

Glory Is Coming!

In the past several years, I have had several dreams of the new creation, of heaven, the time of all consummation, the time when all things will be brought together by God's love. Those dreams were beyond words, but what I most felt in them was a sense of love. They involved going into a place or time that was not foreign, but deeply familiar, where everything was imbued with the presence of God. There was a meeting, a reunion, with that which had been lost, a feeling of old friends and family. It was the world we know now but looked at through God's eternal perspective. In those dreams, I saw hands holding hands and dancing, smiles, laughter, happiness, and all God had created. What was lost was restored. What was forgotten was remembered.

To paraphrase scripture, it is as though Jesus is saying, "My children, I told you I would have a place, a mansion, prepared for you when I called you to my bosom. It is not strange, wild, or unlike earth, but it is rather earth and life living as God would have them—it is as I would have them."

Glory is coming—the new creation, the New Jerusalem. Heaven is rushing toward you. Glory is not streets paved with gold or houses roofed with diamonds. Heaven is a place where your disabilities no longer weigh you down, where sin no longer weighs you down, for your sins are profoundly forgiven by the great Coach of heaven, Jesus. It is in the great and profound moments of everyday existence that you taste the everlasting. It is the healing of this earth, this world, and of glory shining upon the ordinary so that it glows with a divine presence.

Jesus stands ready to take your hand, to infuse you with a wonder, a joy, that makes earthly things and earthly memories pure and touched by the amazement of eternity. It is in the stuff of daily life transfixed and transfigured that heaven will come to be. He can eternally redeem that which was lost and put together what was missing.

Glory, heaven, the new creation, is like seeing again through the eyes of a toddler when everything is utterly fascinating, utterly fresh, and capable of communicating the presence of the light that transforms the ordinary into the holy. Let us therefore see with new eyes. See the depth and the freshness of each smile you see, of each smell you smell, of each taste you taste. Taste the inherent glory that is in those things, for God has given you eyes that can see wonder, eyes that can turn the world into one great astonishment.

Have you ever driven in very high mountains with the mist all around and ached with the beauty that words cannot express? Heaven is life turned into that beauty, real human life as real and earthly as an unconsecrated host and wine, which are then consecrated by glory and become the wondrous drink and meal of the resurrection. Let us abandon ourselves to him, and he will give us a taste of glory.

Pause in Wonder: A Moment with God

Scripture

Then I saw a new heaven and a new earth; for the first heaven and the first earth had passed away, and the sea was no more. And I saw the holy city, the new Jerusalem, coming down out of heaven from God, prepared as a bride adorned for her husband. And I heard a loud voice from the throne saying, "See, the home of God is among mortals.
He will dwell with them;
they will be his peoples,
and God himself will be with them;
he will wipe every tear from their eyes.
Death will be no more;
mourning and crying and pain will be no more,
for the first things have passed away." (Rv 21:1–4, NRSV:CE)

PRAYER

Dear Lord, you dwell in the timelessness of eternity. Even now I can taste that eternity in the Eucharist, in scripture, and in my heart. Make me aware of your nearness and drench me, body and soul, in the everlasting. May the vastness of your caring calm me, soothe me, and fill me with boundless hope. Amen.

REFLECTION

The first time I looked out over the Grand Canyon, its vastness and beauty stunned me. The thought came to me that God is eternally vaster than this canyon, full of boundless love, tender compassion, an eternity of caring.

The statement "God is love" is scriptural, and yet the significance is lost on us because the popular view of love is as sticky sweet, unstable, and mushy as tapioca pudding. Popular songs promote the idea that love is being hooked on feelings. For the statement "God is love" to catch our attention and change us, it must be fleshed out, become everyday, approachable, incarnate. This is exactly what happened at Christmas. The eternal ocean of love that is God became touchable, approachable, real. Infinite, ineffable love became an everyday love—a child in a manger who became a man on a Cross.

In many ways the new creation, heaven, glory, is like a beautiful tapestry. If you look on the back side of a tapestry, all you see are different-colored, dangling strings in no particular order. That's how our lives are. They may be tied and knotted up. They are somewhat incoherent at times. The pattern is not readily available. But if you reverse it and look at the front, you see the beautiful picture depicted by the tapestry. Right now, you see the struggles and the disconnectedness. You see the loose strings. But, in eternity, the tapestry will be turned over, and you will see the front and how it looks from God's eyes. You will see the beautifully woven tapestry forever dwelling in the timelessness of God's eternity.

Starters for Journaling or Meditation

- Have you ever looked out upon the bright stars in the heavens and felt a touch of the everlasting? If so, meditate or write about it.

- When have you had a sense of eternity? Have you ever experienced profound consolation in the midst of loss or deep disappointment? Remember that time and write or meditate about it.

Five

FINDING JOY IN PAIN AND LOSS

The last months of [Kateri's] life are an ever-clearer manifestation of her . . . radiant joy, even in the midst of terrible sufferings. Her last words, simple and sublime, whispered at the moment of her death, sum up, like a noble hymn, a life of purest charity: "Jesus, I love you..."
—JOHN PAUL II, *HOMLIY AT THE BEATIFICATION OF KATERI TEKAKWITHA*

Each of us has had times of loss, times when we passed through the valley of the shadow of death. Maybe it was the loss of a family member, the loss of a childhood, the loss of love. Perhaps you came from a dysfunctional home, or even endured abuse. If we bring Jesus into the process as we face our losses, our hearts can collapse into unspeakable joy. Remembering hand in hand with Jesus can fill our present with wonder.

Real joy means coming to grips with inner pain and loss. Facing our sorrows and losses, grieving, and letting go of the hurt is not a pathway into more sadness but a pathway to unspeakable joy, if we allow ourselves to go through the process. I think of Nicholas Black Elk, the Lakota holy man and Catholic evangelist for whom the bishop of Rapid City, South Dakota, has opened a cause of canonization. Black Elk survived the attempted genocide of his people. He personally survived the horrific massacre of Wounded Knee. In the midst of so much loss to his tribe, he preserved the old Lakota sacred tradition while remaining profoundly Catholic.

People often saw him holding the sacred ceremonial pipe in one hand and the rosary in the other. It is said that he brought four hundred Lakota into the Church. He prayed for people wherever found them, sometimes with the ancient pipe ceremony, sometimes by singing part of the Catholic Mass in Latin. He handled his loss through a depth of prayer, taking the ashes of loss into his hand and giving them to Jesus, by whom they were transformed into boundless joy. His gladness was so infectious that everywhere he traveled people smiled with joy or laughed.

There was a time when I resisted facing great hurt and great pain, blocking off my memories to keep from feeling the depth of my distress. There was a treasure hidden in my heart, but I could not see it until I grieved and let go and finally remembered. Then I was flooded with a richness of memory and an unspeakable joy that sped up my heart as major epiphanies hit.

Pain as a Path to Spiritual Treasure

Black Elk's story reminds me of my grandfather Pop, who, though Cherokee and Baptist, worked through his own ashes to become a true holy man. One phrase that characterized my grandfather would be "joy-bearer." Pop was a bringer of joy, and it was hard to be melancholy in his presence. His eyes would often sparkle and gleam. He was always centered and peaceful; it was so easy for anyone to let down their guard when with him. He had a special kind of peace, a peace under-girded by joy. To him, all creation was baptized in the joy of a loving Creator. All of us were family, God's family: humans, animals, this very earth.

When I was around twelve, I received a great spiritual treasure from my grandfather that to this day continues to inspire awe in me. It came from my grandparents' darkened, cluttered pantry, which was always a mysterious place for me. It not only held foodstuffs, like flour; it held objects from long ago. It is where Pop kept his silver dollars. He knew I loved objects that tied us to the past, and the coins, most minted in the 1800s, did that. Every week without fail, he would go to the pantry, find one, and give it to me. He showed me an old iron mold for making bullets that went back to the nineteenth century. In the pantry, Granny also stored the blackberry wine she made by herself. Though my parents did not know, each time she made a new batch she would give me a sip.

This time, Pop, his eyes wide and glowing, pulled out something from the pantry I had never seen before: a beaded leather belt that had belonged to his full-blooded Cherokee mother, Mary Ensley. Taking it in his hands, he led me back to his chair in the living room and sat me in his chair. He sat on the ottoman facing me. He asked me to stick out my right hand. Then he put his hand on mine, wrapping both of our joined hands in the belt, squeezing in such a way I could not help but feel the bond between us. With happy tears and shining cheeks, he sang some Cherokee hymns—the same hymns his mother had sung to him, when he touched the belt for the first time.[1]

I remained still, almost holding my breath, not wishing to interrupt the surreal moment. Though I did not understand the Cherokee words very well, the sound got deep within me, anointing my soul with profound joy. Tears washed my face too. These were not tears of distress but tears of wonder and connection, a holy joy like the tears that welled up in the eyes of women at the Baptist church when someone came down the aisle to accept Christ.

No, I did not understand all Pop's prayers or hymns, but I knew that something sacred was being passed on to me—a call, a message to share, something from our family, from our ancestors, a call to spiritual manhood. As I reflect on this as an adult, I know what Pop was doing; he knew he would die soon, and he was commissioning me. Much later, on Pentecost Sunday of 2001, the date of my ordination, when Bishop Boland took my hands and encircled them with his stole to tie me to him and his successors, my mind returned to the scene of Pop and the beaded belt.

Pop came down with colon cancer when I was nine. An operation gave him about five more years of life, but it did not get all the cancer. About two months before his death, as I sat on the ottoman and he on his chair with his eyes turned upward to heaven, he said to me, his voice turning wistful, "Eddie, you walk in my soul." This was a special Cherokee way of saying, "I love you." I swallowed hard and said, "Pop, you will always walk in my soul." And he has.

Losing Pop

Pop died when I was thirteen. During those last two or three months, he grew steadily weaker and yellow from jaundice. One day, several weeks before his death, Pop could not get up from his seat. They called Daddy from work, and he carried Pop into the bedroom. I knew that nothing would ever be the same. Pop never came out of that bedroom again alive.

I was terrified to walk into the bedroom and witness Pop dying. I thought if I did not see him anymore, I wouldn't have to think about his dying. He asked for me a number of times, but the horror that had encircled my heart was so fierce that I could not put one wobbly foot in front of the other to go into that room. I knew I was losing Pop, and to keep from feeling that loss and all the turmoil in my family, I did all I could to stop feeling at all.

I was at Granny and Pop's the night he died; Daddy was in the bedroom with Granny and Pop's older granddaughters, Margie and Betty. The preacher was there with him also. I was with the rest of the family gathered in the kitchen area. I felt nothing, just a big blank inside.

Suddenly a shrill scream came from the bedroom; it was Granny. Two other screams came from Margie and Betty. I knew what it meant; Pop had just died. I struggled to find my breath. I fled from it all to the porch, where my Uncle Henry stood, the darkness broken only by the lighted tip of his cigarette. Then the funeral people came and carried Pop's covered body out on a gurney to the hearse. My skin tingled; I was nauseated with a feeling of emptiness. My lips trembled as I pressed them together. I was numb and could not weep.

In order to cope with the enormity of my loss, I stopped thinking about and remembering Pop. Well into my adulthood, I handled the loss and my cowardice of not visiting him in the bedroom the last few weeks of his life by not remembering him. Until I was nearly thirty, every time I drove the turnoff to North Gordon Boulevard, where his cottage had stood, I would shield my vision with my hand to keep from looking at the scene.

In my late twenties, during a time in which I had prayed for many hours to discern more direction in my life, I dreamed a vivid dream, so real I did not know I was dreaming. I was carried in a whirlwind by angels to the bluff above the Chattahoochee to the spot Pop told me was the remembering spot, the spot where he said I could remember him and all he had taught me. In my dream I was terrified; just being there meant facing an ocean of loss and shame. I started thrashing, then awoke in my bed. In the midst of learning the comforting graces of interior prayer, my defenses had begun to break down. I was remembering.

Reclaiming My Memories

Shortly after that dream, Daddy, who at that time was in profound remission from his psychiatric illness, said to me, "Eddie, you are a researcher. You researched Church history; now why not research our family history?"

I knew the time had come. I began to talk with Aunt Nellie, Pop's sister-in-law, who was in her mid-nineties and remembered so much. Aunt Lillian, another of Pop's sisters-in-law, told me about the time she decided to marry Pop's brother Henry. Her father told her she could not marry a "half-breed." But she did anyway and found great joy in this mixed family.

This was just about the time my national ministry had begun. Robert Herrmann and I were invited to give a parish mission in L'Anse, Michigan. Before the mission began, our parish mission host took us out to the nearby Ojibwa Indian reservation church. There we met Fr. John Hascall, O.F.M. Cap., an Ojibwa priest who was also part Cherokee. Not only was he a Catholic pastor representing the Christian tradition; he was the medicine man for his people, representing the Native sacred and cultural tradition.

As I greeted him, I mentioned I had Cherokee heritage and I asked how he could represent both Native and Catholic sacred traditions at the same time. He told me the Gospel expresses itself in the form of the cultures of its people. We call this inculturation, and it is detailed in the Vatican document *Gaudium et Spes*: "From the beginning of her history [the Church] has learned to express the message of Christ. . . . The ability to express Christ's message in its own way is developed in each nation, and at the same time there is fostered a living exchange between the Church and the diverse cultures of people" (44–42). In so doing, the Church has been an instrument of redemption not only for individuals but for whole families and communities as they hear the truth of the Gospel proclaimed into the heart of their lived experience.

"Eddie," Fr. Hascall said, "I meet Native peoples who will never be whole, feel real joy, have their wounds healed, and taste the depths of Jesus' love unless they embrace that healing *as* Native people, allowing him to redeem their sacred cultures." His words went directly to my heart. Listening to him, it seemed that tectonic plates shifted inside me. Fr. Hascall had lit a fuse that I knew would culminate in an eruption.

I did not have to wait long for the eruption. Later that year, Robert Herrmann, Pat Bartholomew (who was then leading retreats with us), and I were on a visit to Pat's parents in Waynesville, in the North Carolina mountains. We drove to the cabin Pop had lived in as a little boy. We pulled up next to the fence that encircled the house and stood there taking pictures. I suddenly felt tons of emotions stir inside me. I collapsed, and these two young and holy men held me as my shoulders quaked with long-suppressed sobs. I was finally grieving for Pop. I stayed there sobbing for twenty minutes as the feeling of loss blended with the subterranean joy that I was finally connecting with Pop again. I could remember Pop now, and a plaintive joy eased into my soul.

Still, on returning home again, I knew there was more. I began to become involved with the Echota Cherokee tribe to which my parents and I belonged. I met with many other Indians at tribal celebrations and at powwows. All carried stories of their families being harassed or rejected because of their heritage. All had joy in their eyes that they had worked this through and come to a place of gladness for their culture and ancestors.

I found out I could only think about Pop a little at a time. Just watching a TV movie about a grandson and his grandfather left me in tears, as did hearing spoken or sung Cherokee. I had always known those memories were there; only now I could take a measured look.

When I was in Thunder Bay, Ontario, leading a retreat for Native people, I saw some old men whose speech and manner reminded me of Pop. Their world was like Pop's world. I made up my mind to face the pain of my early mysteries and make the trip back to the street called North Gordon in Columbus, Georgia. I tried once but met a wall of pain and had to turn back. Then I made a retreat weekend of prayer and rest. I asked God's strength to help me walk down that street once more.

Soon after the retreat, I swallowed hard and headed for North Gordon. I walked slowly up the hill to the bluff above the big river. My limbs wobbled with a blend of reluctance and anticipation, like an Olympic athlete walking expectantly toward the scoreboard or a parent edging toward the nurses' station to see if a beloved daughter pulled through an operation. Dressed in my Native long shirt, I was neither athlete nor grieving parent. I was simply a neurologically impaired person of Native descent, returning for the first time in thirty-five years to the key spot of my childhood, where long ago my soul had been formed. I knew that if I walked those several hundred steps, the world I returned to would forever change.

Walking toward the bluff thrust me into a reality different from the common reality in which we breathe, cry, laugh, and work. I was facing it all now, facing it in one massive encounter. All the things I had for so long wanted to hold back now met me. I had come once before, earlier, but the nausea and resistance had enveloped me, and I had run back to the car, to a safe place. I had not been ready then for what awaited me at the bluff. It would be craziness to run with a raised golf club through a golf course in a thunderstorm. Yet by returning here, I had become a lightning rod for my memories, traditions, and ancestors. But I was not crazy now. I had been crazy to let my heart ever leave this place. I had been crazy to try to erase North Gordon from my soul.

I made my way to the narrow ledge behind the power plant to the remembering spot. So much had happened here long ago. Accepting the memories was a giving up I had long needed. The ledge behind the power plant, partly graded and partly covered with gravel and shiny, broken quartz, provided the surface on which I stood as I looked out over the river. I wore moccasins—what else could I wear on my first trip back?

I felt the gravel and the quartz stone through the leather. My tensions drained away. I wrote the following poem to honor that experience.

> My eyes turned to the water,
> where a Native man emerged,
> the figure of Jesus whom Pop had so loved,
> as though newly baptized by John the Baptist,
> bursting up from the water to the surface

after he had gone under to honor the water.
Before me, filling all from water to sky,
this comfort-bearing face.
How close and familiar was that face.
His eyes soft and filled with an inner glow,
holding his arms out wide as if to hug the world.
How well known were those injured palms.
How many times had I placed my hands in them?
Still, how could you know that face?
How could you touch those palms?
How far could you ever look into those eyes?
This face, so fully Native,
has graced the bare living rooms of so many
who had no other face to turn to for comfort.
Both face and prayer,
some see the face as Caucasian, sometimes as Afri-
     can, sometimes as Asian. I saw it as Indian.
What is the experience of Holy Joy?
but raw awe, mingling with raw comfort,
a mingling that consoles as it enchants.

On my way back from the bluff, back through the corridor to
my car, I stopped by the empty lot where my grandparents'
mill shack had once stood. I faced the river and said a prayer
I had always known.

I honor this water,
I honor this house,
I honor this soil,
I honor the Bible whose words in this place found
     home in the center of my soul,
where long ago my soul was aborning.

I had reached my remembering spot. I knew that after this
experience I would have to speak, shy though I am, about
things private and close. I knew I would have to tell of my

pain, for pain and depths of joy are forever entwined and mutually born from each other.

To do this, I needed more than the encounter with mystery on North Gordon. I needed a human voice to tell me it was time, the voice of an old man who also knew North Gordon's mysteries. His voice alone could tell me when to tell this story. That man was my father.

Good Grief

Before his death in 1996 at age eighty-five, my father told me many of the old stories again, plus some I had never heard before. My father and I drew close during this time. It was as though a cord of joyful brightness tied our two souls together as the grace of the Holy Spirit cascaded over us.

Even so, the telling was hard for him. When he recounted what was good, it meant that he had to remember again what was bad, when he faced real discrimination and prejudice— the times when he was little and the boys taunted him and his full-blooded grandmother, the time racists ran him and his family out of town in Aragon, Georgia, because of their less-than-pure-white pedigree.

Through the years I would often return to North Gordon to sing hymns, experience joy, and remember the things Pop said or did. I discovered that there truly is such a thing as "good grief," as Charlie Brown used to say. I realized that "good grief" is the kind I felt when I faced my worst fear.

When we have experienced acute hurt or loss, it is so easy to soft-pedal the depth of the hurt, to wall it off way deep down inside us where it can turn our whole personality toxic. The answer is to grieve our losses, whatever way is best to us, partly through tears.

Let Mary Guide You

The Blessed Virgin Mary is a beautiful example of pausing in wonder and of finding joy in sorrow. Scripture tells us, "But Mary treasured all these words and pondered them in her heart" (Lk 2:19, NRSV:CE).

She received the wonderful promise of the angel. She experienced the wonder of the birth of her son, Jesus. She thrilled at the miracle in Cana. She heard the preaching of the Kingdom and rejoiced in the feeding of the five thousand. She treasured her memories; she must have swelled with pride in her beloved son.

Then it all fell apart for Mary, as it will all fall apart for each of us at some time in our lives due to hurt or loss. And when it happens, her endurance can be our consolation, her way of sorrows our sure path of hope.

So, what did Mary do when it all fell apart and she found herself in anguish? As the son she so loved was captured, mocked, tortured, and put on a Cross, she remained faithful. Even at the foot of the Cross she remained, grieving, feeling her son's agonies. Despite the torment she suffered, she remained close by, supporting him. What has been called one of the most healing hymns of the Church, the *Stabat Mater*, describes this scene.

> Mary stood grieving, beside the cross weeping,
>   while on it hung [her] son.
> Of all his wounds she felt the smart.
> What pierced his body pierced her heart.
> How grievous was the pain you suffered, O Virgin
>   full of sorrows,
> when you recalled past joys, now all turned to
>   lamentations.[2]

Have you ever seen your joys turn to lamentations? Mary did.

> O Mother, fountain of love, help me feel the power
> of sorrow, that I may grieve with you.

Death and loss were not the final word for Mary, any more than they are the last word for any of us. Resurrection came on the third day, and resurrection can come for us. As the psalmist says, "At dusk weeping comes for the night; but at dawn there is rejoicing" (Ps 30:6).

Pause in Wonder: A Moment with God

SCRIPTURE

I consider that the sufferings of this present time are not worth comparing with the glory about to be revealed to us. For the creation waits with eager longing for the revealing of the children of God; for the creation was subjected to futility, not of its own will but by the will of the one who subjected it, in hope that the creation itself will be set free from its bondage to decay and will obtain the freedom of the glory of the children of God. We know that the whole creation has been groaning in labor pains until now; and not only the creation, but we ourselves, who have the first fruits of the Spirit, groan inwardly while we wait for adoption, the redemption of our bodies. For in hope we were saved. Now hope that is seen is not hope. For who hopes for what is seen? But if we hope for what we do not see, we wait for it with patience. (Rom 8:18–25, NRSV:CE)

PRAYER

Lord, you know my hurt, my losses, and my fragility. Your wounds and your compassion are a salve that heals all pain and loss. You are indeed the God of all comfort. Fill me full of the calm and hope that always comes from beyond. Help me to grieve when I need to grieve, weep when I need to weep; I know that you are near the brokenhearted. At a pace that is right for me, help me to remember the joys and bright threads you have woven into the tapestry of my life. Amen.

REFLECTION

A Jewish parable tells the story of a king who had a beautiful and pure diamond. An accident damaged the diamond, leaving a big scratch. In desperation, the king called for the best diamond-cutters in the realm to restore the diamond. They all said it was not possible; the diamond was scratched beyond repair.

A Jewish lapidary—a pauper at the bottom end of the social ladder—came forward and said he thought he could fix it. A few weeks later he gave the restored diamond back to the king, and it was even more resplendent than before. The lapidary had carved an exquisite rose on the diamond, using the scratch as the stem.

Some impediments, hurts, and losses won't go away, but if we accept what we cannot change and give our sufferings back to God, he can make that which has been damaged and wounded even more beautiful than before. He can rearrange those hurts and transform them into something wondrous.

Because of an as-yet-undiagnosed learning disability, I made two unsatisfactory grades in my final year of Protestant seminary and was asked to leave. I felt utterly lost and directionless. A priest friend of mine came to me at my lowest point, put his hand on my shoulder, and said, "Eddie, you may not see it now, but you are going to be of great service to the Church; trust me." His words made me feel found and, as it turned out, I was able to be of service to the Church. Jesus turned the world's understanding of things upside down, seeking the lost and forgotten. His Father loved with a scandalous love—prostitutes, drunkards, tax collectors were special objects of his passionate caring. By the way Jesus lived his life, he showed what God was like, reaching out to people in the deepest level of their lostness, loving the undeserving, turning lives around. He can change our lives, too, when we feel lost and alone. The presence of his love in our souls can help us decide to turn toward grace and change, when we need to change.

Starters for Journaling or Meditation

- Do you have a "remembering place"? How has remembering—perhaps with another person—helped you to pause in wonder and experience joy even in sorrow? Write or meditate on this.

- Think of a time you experienced "good grief," or consolation in the midst of loss. What was that like? What part did God have in it? Write or meditate on this.

Six

FINDING JOY IN SINGING WITH THE ANGELS

Suddenly new joyful sounds emerged from people.
—St. Augustine of Hippo[1]

One of the happiest discoveries in my life has been an ancient form of prayer that offers a foretaste of heaven, a way of opening up so God can fill us with boundless joy. Great theologians like St. Thomas Aquinas and St. Augustine prayed this way. Great spiritual leaders like St. Francis prayed this way. Countless numbers of Christians prayed this way in the first fifteen centuries of the history of the Church, and now this prayer form is experiencing a resurgence of interest through the renewal movement. It has brightened my life and the lives of thousands of other Christians, knitting together the souls of all God's people—Catholic, Protestant, and Orthodox alike.

This simple way of prayer can transfigure our lives, just as it transfigured the lives of the apostles at the birthday of the Church. We get a hint of it in the book of Ephesians, where St. Paul writes: "And do not get drunk on wine, in which lies debauchery, but be filled with the Spirit, addressing one another [in] psalms and hymns and spiritual songs, singing and playing to the Lord in your hearts" (Eph 5:18–19).

In the book of Revelation, the apostle John gives us a glimpse of the heavenly throne room in which the angels and saints worship (see Rv 7). Have you ever wondered what it would be like to hear angels singing? Have you ever wanted to enter into the heavenly chorus and sing along with them? This is the ancient prayer form that is sometimes called "singing with the angels," a form of worship that flows from a heart of love (see 1 Cor 13:1).

I experienced this gift for the first time one evening by myself in a hotel room, when the Holy Spirit unexpectedly guided my voice into a kind of wordless song; I had the strong sense that I was harmonizing with the sounds of heaven. Then the next evening I was in a group of people whose voices, mysteriously and spontaneously it seemed, burst forth with a similar song that seemed straight from on high. As I sang with them, a delight rushed from deep down inside to my heart and voice, bringing me to a place of utter joy. Those sounds liberated me, pushing away the dejection, inertia, and despair. It was clear that God's mighty joy was at work in me and those around us.

I later learned that what I had experienced was commonly experienced by millions of Christians worldwide and a way of prayer for both average believers and saints of the Catholic Church for over a millennium and a half. One of the words, the most common word in Catholic history, to describe this is the word *jubilation* from the Latin word *jubilatio* meaning a wordless call or "whoop."[2]

In a recent article on jubilation in *Commonweal*, Joseph A. Komonchak asserts that this kind of wordless praise has deep roots: "The verb *jubilo* and the noun *jubilatio* occur often in the Psalms. . . . Augustine would point out that the word referred to a vocal expression used to express a joy or happiness too immense or too deep for words."[3] In the article he specifically references Augustine's commentary on Psalm 99 (100):2 ("Whoop to God, all the earth...") and Psalm 88-89:16 ("Blessed is the people that understands whooping").[4] Komonchak quotes from Augustine's commentary on Psalm 46 as follows:

> What I am about to say you already know.
> One who is whooping does not speak words. Whooping is a certain sound of joy without words; it's the sound of a mind poured forth in joy, expressing an affection, as far as possible . . . a sound of exultation without words.[4]

Singing in the Spirit: A Gateway to Joy

Let me take you back to the first time I encountered this prayer form. I was studying to be a Presbyterian minister and had begun preaching weekends in Presbyterian churches all over Texas. Already my heart was growing steadily Catholic, but I was not yet ready to change my course.

One night I was alone in a motel room in rural Texas; I was to preach the next day at a Sunday service in a nearby Presbyterian church. I was knotted up inside, and I found it impossible to pray. There were many reasons I was so conflicted. I was studying at a Presbyterian seminary with high academic requirements. My brain dysfunction left me with many visual-spatial problems: I had illegible handwriting, a limited ability to type with an old-fashioned typewriter, and attention problems that kept me from staying focused in class. I felt crushed by an elephantine academic weight.

In addition, I struggled with the calling I felt to become a Catholic. The Presbyterian Church had been good to me. I loved much of Reformed theology, especially the writings of Karl Barth. I had served as a summer student pastor and preached on weekends at Presbyterian churches that did not have a pastor. The struggle to decide which faith community to give my life to drained me and left me paralyzed.

In that situation I did what most Protestant preachers would do when confronted with such major stress: I started to thumb through the Bible.

My eyes fell on a passage in St. Paul that said when we do not know how to pray as we ought, the Spirit prays through us in sighs too deep for words. I read, "Likewise the Spirit helps us in our weakness; for we do not know how to pray as we ought, but that very Spirit intercedes with sighs too deep for words. And God, who searches the heart, knows what is the mind of the Spirit, because the Spirit intercedes for the saints according to the will of God" (Rom 8:26–27, NRSV:CE).

That is what I need, I thought, *the Spirit praying through me.* Without thinking, I began to sigh. As the scripture suggested, I invited the Holy Spirit to intercede for me. I gave control of my voice to God. Gradually the sighs changed into comforting, joyous songs without words. I was overwhelmed and moved to tears by their beauty.

For thirty minutes I lay there peacefully in the stillness, as waves of divine love coursed through me. When my praying in this unique "language" was finished, I rested in the stillness of God. The next morning people responded to my sermon in a way I had not seen congregations react to my words before.

On the way back to my seminary, I began to think of the experience. Was this what one of my professors, also a leader in the charismatic renewal, called "praying in tongues"? I had earlier read an article by Kilian McDonnell, O.S.B., on the charismatic renewal in the Catholic Church, and was theoretically aware of the supernatural gifts of the Spirit, especially tongues. I had one professor, Dr. J. Rodman Williams (we called him Rod), who held a prayer meeting in his home every Sunday night. I thought for a moment that I ought to go to that evening's prayer meeting. Maybe the people there could help me understand my experience.

Almost immediately, I tried to talk myself out of it as reality crashed in. Entering the door of Rod's home would brand me at the seminary. I would be "one of those" and that brand could affect my future as a Presbyterian minister. Almost the entire faculty of the seminary ardently opposed Rod; they took notice when a student started attending his prayer meeting. With everything else going on in my life, I didn't want to draw any more attention to myself.

Ultimately I decided to attend the prayer group that night, though I continued to have ambivalent feelings about it. About thirty-five people from all over the city of Austin attended that meeting, as well as two or three students from the Presbyterian seminary. About ten of the people came from St. Edward's University, a Holy Cross university in Austin.

As people prayed and sang wordlessly in the living room, beatific happiness beamed brightly from everyone's face. Some sang spontaneously with fresh words and melodies of the heart given at the moment by the Spirit. A wondrous harmonious melody like angels singing filled the room. I joined my voice with theirs. Later I was to learn that harmonious singing was a way of prayer found in the Catholic tradition called "jubilation" (*jubilatio* in Latin), which modern-day charismatics called "singing in tongues."

Afterward, Rod and his wife, Jo, gave me a wholehearted hug. As they prayed over me for a further release of the Spirit, I felt showered by the very presence of God as the love of new brothers and sisters surrounded me. I left feeling energized and at peace.

The Jubilation of the Saints

My early discovery of tongues/jubilation and the immense joy I experienced reminds me of an early description of St. Francis praying in jubilation. The practice and use of jubilation among the early Franciscans was widespread.[5] One of Francis's earliest biographers, Br. Leo, writes in his book *The Mirror of Charity (Speculum Perfectionis)*:

> Francis prayed in jubilation with great spontaneity, "Intoxicated by love and compassion for Christ, Blessed Francis sometimes used to act like this. For the sweetest of spiritual melodies would often well up within him and found expression in French sound, and the murmurs of God's voice, heard by him alone, would joyfully pour forth in French-like jubilations."[6]

The New Testament presents tongues as a gift of speaking that could be heard by people of different languages as well as a person or group praying too rich and too deep for words, a "praying in the Spirit." The gift of tongues is a kind of non rational prayer of the heart, a gift of praying and praising God aloud but without intelligible words (see 1 Cor 12:10; 14:5; cf. Rom 8:26–27). Some thought the sounds to be the sound and language of angels. First Corinthians 13:1 suggests this when it speaks of the tongues of angels. The gift is also seen as entering into the unspeakable wonder of God—as Paul describes it, "speaking mysteries in the Spirit" (1 Cor 14:2b, NRSV:CE).

Tongues and jubilation as prayer are almost certainly related to praying in "angelic languages," which was a part of the Judaism of Christ's time. Because Paul speaks of the tongues of angels (see 1 Cor 13:1), this form of prayer was likely part of the earliest Christian liturgy. *Angelglossy* is the name given to this Jewish practice.[7] Many scholars believe jubilation was practiced in New Testament times as a continuation of praying in the Spirit (in tongues). Also, the often-detailed accounts of jubilation in the spiritual history of the Church hardly differ from what is called tongues in the modern-day Church. Hear what Augustine says about jubilation:

> He who sings a *jubilus* does not utter words; he pronounces a wordless sound of joy; the voice of his soul pours forth happiness as intensely as possible, expressing what he feels without reflecting on any particular meaning; to manifest his joy, the man does not use words that can be pronounced and understood, but he simply lets his joy burst forth without words; his voice then appears to express a happiness so intense that he cannot formulate it.[8]

Augustine describes a Mass he celebrated in his home church in Hippo when two people were healed of palsy. Here are Augustine's words describing the holy chaos of joy in his parish church.

The exultation continued, and the wordless praise
to God was shouted so loud that my ears could
scarcely stand the din. But, of course, the main
point was, in the hearts of this clamoring crowd,
there burned that faith in Christ for which the
martyr Stephen shed his blood.[9]

A Closer Look at Jubilation

My professor Rod Williams, who later became a renowned
theologian at Regent University, knew I would want to
understand more of this experience, and he started me on
an academic study and research plan that eventually led to
my first book, on the topic of jubilation. Surprisingly, instead
of leading me deeper into the Presbyterian tradition, this
experience felt profoundly Catholic.

The passage of years and hundreds of hours spent in
research showed me just how profoundly Catholic it was. For
example, St. Thomas Aquinas highlighted the importance of
praying out loud to engage the emotions, making jubilation
part of the prayer:

First, [praying aloud] is a way in which we can stir
ourselves with our words to pray with devotion.
Secondly, praying aloud can keep our attention
from wandering, because we can concentrate better if we support our feelings with words when we
pray . . . when our mind is kindled by devotion as
we pray, we break out spontaneously into weeping
and sighing and cries of jubilation and other such
noises . . . we have to serve the God to whom we
offer reverence in prayer not only with our minds,
but also with our bodies.[10]

Aquinas's earliest biographer, Bernard Gui, gives vivid description of this kind of vocal, emotional, and charismatic prayer.

Gui describes a scene when Thomas was teaching in Paris on Paul's writings and came to a difficult passage to interpret. He ordered his secretaries out of the room, "fell to the ground and prayed with tears,—then what he desired was given him and it all became clear."[11] Such a catharsis—letting emotions out through jubilation, tears, fervent prayer, and cries—attuned him to the spiritual world, and visions guided him at times in his groundbreaking teaching.

As part of my discovery of the Catholic Church, I read the early Fathers and Mothers of the Church and the original lives of the saints, especially St. Francis. The description of thousands of people praying in jubilation and the genuinely felt emotion in their worship was far richer than what I had seen at modern-day charismatic Masses and prayer groups.

One of the most exquisite accounts of group jubilation in the Spirit ever written is the account by Thomas of Celano of the canonization of Francis. (This is a firsthand account; he was doubtless present at the canonization.) The life of Francis had been like a lyric poem. His love, his strength, and his tenderness had touched tens of thousands before his death. Celano in his book *Early Francisan Classics*:

> People danced in the streets. . . . The crowd of people marked the occasion "with great jubilation, and the brightness of the day was made brighter by the torches they brought." . . . The Pope was so moved by that he "breathed deep sighs that rose from the bottom of his heart," and, seeking relief in repeated sobs (of joy), he shed a torrent of tears. The other prelates of the Church likewise poured forth a flood of tears, so that their sacred vestments were dampened by the abundant flow. Then all the people began to weep (for joy).[12]

As the pope lifted up his hands to heaven and proclaimed Francis enrolled among the saints, Celano writes:

> At these words the reverend cardinals, together with the Lord Pope, began to sing the *Te Deum* in a loud voice. Then there was raised a clamor among the many people praising God: the earth resounded with their mighty voices, the air was filled with their jubilations, and the ground was moistened with their tears. New songs were sung, and the servants of God jubilated in melody of the Spirit. Sweet sounding organs were heard there, and spiritual hymns were sung with well-modulated voices. There a very sweet odor was breathed, and a most joyous melody that stirred the emotions resounded there.[13]

This passage from Celano's book, in which the crowd jubilates in "melody of the Spirit," reinforces the idea that we can allow the Holy Spirit to guide our voices in prayer, which in turn can lead to spontaneous songs in our own language or in jubilation.

After reading this account of Celano, I went further with my research and found hundreds of references to emotionally expressive worship and jubilation in the tradition of the Church. In fact, as the word *jubilation* was used through the centuries, it came to include not just wordless songs but most emotional expressions of private prayer or group prayer.

Congregations expressed their yearning for God in wordless singing. Though not much research has been done on this aspect of early devotion, we do have the work of medieval music historians on jubilation. These music historians have studied it intensely as they investigated the roots of Western music. Albert Seay, a modern music historian, beautifully describes musical jubilation as "an overpowering expression of the ecstasy of the spirit, a joy that could not be restricted to words; it . . . occupied a peculiar place in the liturgy, for it carried implications of catharsis, a cleansing of the soul."[14]

Another major work dealing with the jubilus in detail, *Les Peres de l'Eglise et la Musique*, emphasizes its improvised nature: "One notes the more or less spontaneous impulse (of the jubilus). . . . In (these jubilations) they exhaled joy to some extent without control."[15]

Though praying in jubilation as a regular part of the liturgy diminished as the number of people converting to Christianity swelled, it continued as a form of private prayer and small-and large-group prayer until the sixteenth century. Large groups, as shown by the earlier descriptions of the canonization of St. Francis, could still pray in the Spirit.

Jubilation and Contemplative Prayer

Jubilation is forever married with joy and wonder. Singing in jubilation is a way of giving oneself over to an expression of the richest joy.

Like contemplation, it involves letting go of control and allowing the Holy Spirit to pray through us. In contemplative prayer, we rest in the stillness of the love of God. We will speak more of this kind of prayer in the chapter on developing a contemplative heart. Contemplation enables us to recline on God's bosom as our hearts unwind from the often-tangled busyness of the day to the quiet of a child resting in its mother's lap (see Ps 131).

When associated with contemplation, jubilation settles into a soft, quiet, almost whispering sound. A wonderful account of praying this way is found in the earliest stories of St. Francis recorded in the *Little Flowers of St. Francis*. Masseo, one of Francis's closest companions, prayed that way. Here is a quote, which is translated from the original Italian:

> And Brother Masseo remained so filled with the grace of the desired virtue of humility and with the light of God that from then on he was in jubilation all the time. And often when he was praying . . . he would make a jubilus that sounded like the cooing of a gentle dove, "Ooo–Ooo–Ooo." And with a joyful expression, he would remain in contemplation in that way. . . . Brother James of Fallerone asked him why he didn't change the intonation in his jubilation. And he (Masseo) answered very joyfully: "Because when we have found all that is good in one thing, it is not necessary to change the intonation."[16]

I remember an elderly man, Bob, who attended one of our retreats many years ago. He and his wife had been fervent charismatics, and often prayed loudly in public. Then his wife was gravely injured in a car accident. There were many internal injuries; her liver was cut, her spleen torn. The doctor gave Bob a 2 percent chance she could survive the surgery. After she went into surgery, Bob nearly ran to the hospital chapel and sat before the tabernacle.

As his tears flowed, Bob wondered if he should shout out in a jubilation begging God's mercy. Somehow it didn't seem right. Then it was almost as though God spoke to his heart, "This is a time for you to grow still and whisper." He then began to pray a soft jubilus, just quietly mouthing and whispering a soothing jubilus. As he did, he sank into the stillness of the comfort of God's embrace.

He lost track of time, and two hours passed. Then he went back to the surgery waiting room, and soon the doctor, in surgery scrubs, came back to get him. "The surgery went well, better than we dared expect. She has a rough road ahead of her, though." To the great surprise of her doctors, after a grueling three months in the hospital, Bob's wife made a full recovery. And Bob discovered the gift of contemplative prayer.

In my own life, I have found that when I use the Jesus Prayer, a short repetitive prayer around the name of Jesus, to anchor me in the stillness, I often switch back and forth between the Jesus Prayer and praying a soft jubilus. I have found this a wonderful way of disposing my heart to the gift of contemplation.

St. Teresa of Avila and the Jubilus

Praying in jubilation can also tie together the hearts of a handful of people. An illustration of this is found in the early literature about St. Teresa of Avila, the great Catholic mystic and contemplative. Expressive worship in the Spirit, and singing in the Spirit, played a significant part of the prayer life of her Carmelite community, leading to a transcendent state of bliss and well-being.

Dance also played a significant part in the prayer of Teresa and her sisters. Says author Marcelle Auclair:

> For Teresa of Jesus, tenderness and gaiety were such innocent manifestations of the love of one's neighbor and thus of the love of God that even at recreation, fervor took possession and she became incapable of resisting the urge of the spirit. She

would begin to dance, turning round and round
and clapping her hands as King David danced
before the ark; the nuns accompanied her "in a
perfect transport of spiritual joy."[17]

Later, when some of her nuns went to France to found Carmelite convents there, the French nuns, to their great surprise,
saw the mother superior "more like a seraphim than a mortal
creature executing a sacred dance in the choir, singing and
clapping her hands in the Spanish way, but with so much
dignity, sweetness and grace, that, filled with holy reverence,
they felt themselves wholly moved by divine grace and their
hearts raised to God."[18]

It is interesting to note that the dancing was, at times, done
"in choir"—that is, in the context of the Divine Office, thus
having a liturgical setting. Teresa and her nuns could be overwhelmed by the spiritual power of improvised singing. One
Easter, Teresa asked one of the nuns to sing an improvised
song. She sang: "May my eyes behold thee, good and sweet
Jesus . . . Let him who will, delight his gaze with jasmine and
with roses. If I were to see thee, a thousand gardens would lie
before my eyes."[19] Teresa was so overwhelmed with this song
that she fell unconscious in ecstasy. When she came to, she
herself sang an improvised song (in the Spirit). From then on
when she would go into ecstasy, her nuns would surround her
and sing softly.[20]

So we see in Teresa and her nuns refreshing examples of
not only expressive worship, but group sharing in prayer and
mystical experience. The expressive and spontaneous prayer
experiences Teresa and her nuns had as a group show us that
even at this late date mysticism could still be tied to warm
group prayer experiences.

How to Enter into the Wonder of Jubilation

Jubilation is a way of attuning our hearts to the joyful song of God himself. In timeless imagery, St. Peter Chrysologus associates the word *jubilation* with the call of a shepherd. He pictures Jesus as the shepherd that calls the sheep by means of the shepherd's yodel, the jubilation. Chrysologus breaks into poetry as he describes the call of the shepherd:

> The Shepherd with sweet jubilus, with varied melody, leads the flock to pasture, keeps the tired flock at rest under shaded grove. This jubilus urges the flock to climb lofty mountains, there to graze on healthful grasses. Also it calls them to descend to the low valleys slowly and without hurry. How happy are those sheep that join their voices to the voice of the Shepherd, that follow when he calls to feed and gather. They truly jubilate to their Shepherd . . . let us jubilate.[21]

Jubilation is a means of uniting with God's own song, yodeling back and forth tenderly to the one who loves us most. It is a treasure that once enlivened the whole Church. It can become that again.

Jubilation came with Pentecost, equipping God's people with a great tool of prayer that leads to immense joy that can be God's means of healing us and tuning us into the wonder of the heartbeat of heaven. That gift is available to all who ask in faith. You can find out more about the gift of jubilation by getting in touch with a charismatic prayer group in your area, or by taking a Life in the Spirit seminar.[22] Finally, ask the Holy Spirit to give you this gift, so that you might worship with renewed joy. As Pope St. John XXIII prayed at the beginning of the Second Vatican Council, "Renew your wonders in our time, as though by a new Pentecost."[23] You can pray for wonders to be renewed in your own life, too, including the gift of jubilation.

Pause in Wonder: A Moment with God

SCRIPTURE

Likewise the Spirit helps us in our weakness; for we do not know how to pray as we ought, but that very Spirit intercedes with sighs too deep for words. And God, who searches the heart, knows what is the mind of the Spirit, because the Spirit intercedes for the saints according to the will of God. (Rom 8:26–27, NRSV:CE)

As you sing psalms and hymns and spiritual songs among yourselves, singing and making melody to the Lord in your hearts. . . . (Eph 5:19, NRSV:CE)

Let the word of Christ dwell in you richly; teach and admonish one another in all wisdom; and with gratitude in your hearts sing psalms, hymns, and spiritual songs to God. (Col 3:16, NRSV:CE)

PRAYER
Traditional Holy Spirit Prayer

> Come, Holy Spirit, Creator come,
> From your bright heavenly throne!
> Come, take possession of our souls,
> And make them all your own.
> You who are called the Paraclete,
> Best gift of God above,
> The living spring, the living fire,
> Sweet unction, and true love!
> Amen.[24]

A Prayer for a Release of the Spirit

Use this prayer (or your own words) to invite the Holy Spirit to be released in your life.

> Dear Lord, send your Spirit of power and love upon me. Release in me your Spirit as in a new Pentecost. Infuse me with love and power and bestow on me all the fruits and gifts of the Spirit. Open me to the miraculous workings of the Spirit and a spirit of calm and peace. Help me to praise you both loudly and, at times, softly. Dear Lord, turn my breath and vocal cords into a lyre of the Spirit. Dear Spirit, guide my voice into wondrous joy.
>
> Dear Lord, please give me the gift of jubilation, singing, and praying in tongues. Amen.

Begin praising and thanking God in your own language spontaneously. Open your mouth, beginning with the syllable *ah*. Begin to turn your voice over to the Holy Spirit. Let him guide your voice.

REFLECTION

Are you hesitant to try to "sing with the angels" with this form of jubilant prayer? It is remarkable to see how the Holy Spirit can use this kind of prayer to restore the joy of those who are struggling, those who have lost their joy.

I remember a time when attending a prayer conference offered by the Alleluia Community. I was riding in a car with a young teen who was traveling with the group from my parish. It was clear that he was deeply depressed. His eyes were downcast, and his facial muscles were motionless. As the conference was about to begin, I asked him what was wrong, and he muttered, "My girlfriend of a year broke up with me for another boy. Now no one will ever love me like she did. As far as I am concerned, my life is over at sixteen."

I didn't press further but decided to let the Spirit do the healing for him as the conference unfolded. As we prayed together in a large group between conference talks, his facial expression slowly changed to a more normal appearance. He looked us in the eye rather than looking downward. At the last Mass of the conference, people began to sing loudly with joyful jubilations and arms raised wide and outward as though to embrace heaven. The young man, tears streaming down his face, joined jubilation for the first time, raising and clapping his hands, swaying with the movements of the jubilus and the Spirit. Afterward, he seemed like a changed child, full of gladness and ready to embrace his future. Jubilation can work miracles like this.

Prayers of praise chase away sadness and gloom. God doesn't need compliments; prayers of praise are for *our* sake. In praise, we lose ourselves in wonder. It helps us glimpse the glory of God and the glory of his creation. It lifts our spirits as we touch unfathomable grandeur and love.

Starters for Journaling or Meditation

- Remember times you praised God through singing hymns, reciting psalms, or speaking to God directly in conversational prayer. If you cannot recall such a time, try it each day for a week, and write about your experiences.

- How do you think the gift of jubilation helped saints like St. Francis and St. Teresa of Avila to grow in holiness? How might it enhance your ability to pray in wonder? Write or meditate about it.

Seven

FINDING JOY
IN SCRIPTURE

"Among the many fruits of this biblical springtime I would like to mention the spread of the ancient practice of lectio divina or "spiritual reading" of Sacred Scripture . . . . that it may nourish meditation and contemplation and, like water, succeed in irrigating life itself."
—BENEDICT XVI, *ANGELUS*, NOVEMBER, 2005

God comes to us not only in visions and spiritual experiences, but also in scripture. Scripture can fill our hearts with the wondrous presence behind scripture. I learned of the power of Jesus to reach through scripture from my Aunt Genella and Uncle Guthrie.

My Aunt Genella Crittenden played a vital role in shaping my spiritual life. She was a devout Baptist, raised in the parsonage of the Baptist church in Odem, Georgia, where her father was the minister. Her love of Christ and the scriptures came from deep within her. I have a vivid memory of the summer I was nine, spending two weeks with her and her husband, my Uncle Guthrie.

When I came to them, I was as frightened and stressed out as a nine-year-old boy could be. My father's mental illness was in remission for a while, but my mother was suffering from a stomach condition and depression; her weight had plummeted from her normal 130 pounds to a gaunt 96. Aunt Lovey had died several months before, and now I feared losing my mother. I was also heavily burdened with the shame from my own mysterious, undiagnosed disability—I could not escape the symptoms, feeling constantly confused, clumsy, and awkward.

Earlier that year I had seen some awful cartoons that depicted God sending children to hell to be terrorized by demons. Those movies terrified me, and I lived in constant fear that God would send me to hell also because I was clumsy and awkward and not good with everyday tasks.

A short time later, I suffered added trauma while driving home one day with Uncle Guthrie and one of my cousins through Birmingham, Alabama; we witnessed a man crossing the street being hit by an oncoming car. I still remember the blood gushing from his head as he lay dying on the pavement.

All these disquieting events weighed heavily upon me. I was terrified of my mother dying. I shook inside with the prospect of being sent to hell. Scenes of the man bleeding on the pavement flashed before my eyes, followed by scenes of my dying in the same manner. Like most nine-year-olds, I kept most of this to myself. Finally, one night as I lay in bed, tossing with worry, it became too much for me to handle alone. I had to tell.

Hesitantly, I made my way to Aunt Genella and Uncle Guthrie's bedroom and gently knocked on the door. When my aunt finally opened the door, I blurted, "I'm sure I'm going to hell."

She listened patiently, and the words continued to pour out of me as I named my other fears: of my mother dying, and of my own death, and of the nightmares I'd had about that pedestrian in Birmingham. Aunt Genella lovingly motioned for me to climb onto their bed where I sat nestled securely between them, my back propped up against the headboard with a pillow.

Their voices were full of warmth and comfort. First, they assured me that God loved me and was not sending me to hell. Aunt Genella pulled out their large family Bible, then slowly and tenderly, pausing often, she read passages from scripture that soothed and comforted. Fifty years later, I still recall those verses.

> Ask, and it will be given you; search, and you will find; knock, and the door will be opened for you. For everyone who asks receives, and everyone who searches finds, and for everyone who knocks, the door will be opened. Is there anyone among you who, if your child asks for bread, will give a stone? Or if the child asks for a fish, will give a snake? If you then, who are evil, know how to give good gifts to your children, how much more will your Father in heaven give good things to those who ask him! (MT 7:7–11, NRSV:CE)

After reading the passage, Aunt Genella said, "Eddie, by coming in here tonight, you are asking and seeking. Your heavenly Father won't respond by giving you a snake or a stone, or by sending you to hell. Tonight he offers you his comfort and peace." Then she opened her Bible again and began calmly reading one scripture verse after another. Aunt Genella's slow reading of scripture wove a web of safety around my soul.

My stress and worries didn't go away completely overnight, though I began to feel joy returning as my aunt and uncle continued to pray and read to me. That calming time with Aunt Genella and the Bible was like the Mount of Transfiguration for me. In the holy light of the scriptures, my fears diminished, and I tasted something of the glory of God. The world seemed different, even wondrous, afterward.

Later in my life, I discovered that the slow, prayerful way Aunt Genella read scripture with pauses was similar to a traditional Catholic way of praying scripture called *lectio divina,* which opens our hearts to the embrace of God. The scriptures can astound us with God's power to lighten and brighten us.[1]

What Is *Lectio Divina*?

Lectio divina is a Latin term that means "divine reading." This is spiritual reading that is very different from Bible study, when we read scripture to obtain knowledge and meaning, consider it in context, and often consult good commentaries. Lectio divina is a different, more intimate reading of scripture, a reading with the heart. Lectio divina is also a way of prayerfully listening for the soft, quiet voice of God— a voice that can lead us to the joy of wonderment. St. Benedict called lectio divina listening "with the ear of our heart."

The origins of lectio divina may be traced back to the Jewish veneration of the Torah. The ancient roots of lectio divina are found in a Hebrew method of studying scripture called "Haggadah," a process of learning through the heart, as Carl Arico explains in *A Taste of Silence*:

> [Haggadah] was an interactive interpretation of the Scriptures by means of the free use of the text to explore their inner meaning. It was part of the devotional practice of the Jews in the days of Jesus. The Jews would memorize the text in a process that involved repeating the passage over and over softly with the lips until the words themselves gradually took up residence in the heart, there transforming the person's life.[2]

Hebrew scholars would first memorize passages of the sacred text, then repeat them over and over again, slowly and softly, until the words made a home in the heart, transforming and gladdening the whole person. The psalmist would seem to be describing this process in Psalm 119: "How sweet are your words to my taste, sweeter than honey to my mouth! . . . Your word is a lamp to my feet and a light to my path" (vv. 103, 105, NRSV:CE).

We find a very similar approach to engaging the scriptures in the ancient Christian practice of lectio divina, a practice that we find first mentioned in the writings of the Church Fathers and Mothers of the third century, in the early years of monastic life in the desert. St. Benedict of Nursia referenced it in his famous Rule: "Listen readily to holy reading, and devote yourself often to prayer."[3] In the twelfth century, a Carthusian monk named Guigo composed a book, *The Ladder of Monks*, outlining the four steps typically associated with this spiritual practice: *lectio* (reading), *oratio* (prayer), *meditatio* (meditation), and *contemplatio* (contemplation).

We will explore these in greater depth a bit later—but first I want to tell you about my friend, Lucille, who has a powerful testimony about how embracing lectio divina can help you to engage the scriptures with greater wonder and joy.

Learning to Communicate with God

A year after the death of her husband, Lucille was still in the grip of crisis. She and her husband had both been in their sixties when he died. For two decades they had been active in Marriage Encounter and helped hundreds of couples to learn good marital communication techniques at retreat weekends. Their work with Marriage Encounter deepened the bond of love they shared together, and her husband's death devastated Lucille, who had never thought about or planned for living alone.

She found that praying was especially difficult; she and her husband had always spent their quiet times together, and she was not used to praying alone. She carried a weight of grief and stress. One day Lucille read about lectio divina in a magazine, and she decided to try it. She picked a passage from Isaiah 40 and slowly began reading to herself, savoring each word.

> Comfort, comfort my people, says your God. Speak tenderly to Jerusalem, and cry to her that her warfare is ended. (Is 40:1–2, ESV)

Lucille read the passage two or three times slowly before something truly touched her: "Speak tenderly to Jerusalem . . ." Softly she began repeating the phrase. "Speak tenderly to Jerusalem . . ." Gradually she felt led to shorten the phrase, praying, "Speak tenderly . . . speak tenderly . . . speak tenderly." A gentle love quietly welled up within her.

Anyone who has been in love knows that there are moments of wordless communion when hearts seem as one, resting together in the silence of that love. Lucille recognized that sense of utter peace as she continued to meditate upon that phrase: "Speak tenderly to me, O Lord. Speak tenderly to me." She slowly repeated that prayer until her heart quieted. She then rested in the silence for five or ten minutes.

Later, she said to me, "Praying that scripture helped me to feel, for the first time since my husband died, that God loved me tenderly." As she daily prayed this way, an abiding sense of God's presence filled her heart.

Of course, lectio divina did not take away the pain from the loss of her husband, but it did give her a sense that when she prayed, she was not alone. "I know I will always grieve for him until my own death," she said to me. "But I know for sure now that there is indeed someone who holds me close besides my husband. God is someone who can dance and sing within me and give me a taste of heavenly joy. And I can converse with him at any moment and let God gladden me through scripture."

Lectio Divina for Groups

While lectio divina is primarily for individual prayer, it can also be adapted for use by groups. Twenty years ago, I personally saw God use lectio divina to change a school faculty from gloom to gladness.

For a full week I had dreaded giving a retreat to the faculty of a midwestern Catholic girls' school. It was a last-minute booking, and when the pastor called to invite me, he warned me that the faculty was in a meltdown. The new principal had been pushing the teachers hard to improve their teaching skills and lesson plans. Some of the teachers were feeling resentful; a few were even insubordinate. What could I say to them? God only knew.

I kept hoping they would cancel, but they didn't. Five minutes into my first talk of the morning, I knew the retreat was in trouble. Grim, stony faces glared at me. The audience reminded me of a pot of water on the edge of boiling over. Rumors (which turned out to be unfounded) had circulated that the board was going to fire several of the teachers or replace the principal. During lunch break, a handful of teachers on both sides of the dispute unburdened themselves to me.

I had planned to give a talk on prayer for the first afternoon conference. However, given the current state of the faculty, I doubted the talk would be well received. As I mulled over what to present in that afternoon conference, I remembered how Aunt Genella's prayerful reading of scripture had encircled me in calm and safety when I was nine. Suddenly, it came to me: We didn't need to talk *about* prayer; we needed to *pray*. Most of all, we needed to pray scripture.

That afternoon we needed words and thoughts from beyond ourselves to penetrate our hearts. I first gave a brief introduction to lectio divina. Next, I asked everyone to close their eyes. I began playing a CD of the slow, prayerful Pachelbel's "Canon in D" in the background. After the music had played for a minute or two, we took about ten minutes to say the Jesus Prayer. In the calm and quiet, I slowly started reading from 1 Corinthians 13, pausing in the stillness when I felt the gentle touch of the Spirit move over the group. It was clear from their faces that the group was settling into a deep state of prayer.

When I finished reading the chapter the first time, I went back and read it again, slowly and with pauses, giving time for the words to sink in. This time I repeated words and phrases that seemed "anointed" by a special touch of the Spirit. "Love is patient," I repeated slowly, then paused in a long silence. "Love is kind. It is not irritable or resentful." I paused again.

Next I read from the thirteenth chapter of the Gospel of John, the passage that describes Jesus washing the feet of the disciples. In the second reading of the passage, I slowly repeated the phrase "wash one another's feet." When I had finished the reading, we took ten minutes of silent prayer. After a few moments, one of the middle-aged teachers spontaneously broke the quiet. Tears coursing down her face, her voice choked as she addressed the group. "I regret so much my outburst at the last faculty meeting." She turned to the principal, saying, "You didn't deserve the cruel words I aimed at you. You are a decent human being who loves the students as much as I do."

The principal walked over and embraced the teacher, tears streaming from her eyes, too. The principal addressed the group as well. "Please forgive me. I could certainly be far more sensitive to your feelings and opinions as I implement these new policies." Then one teacher after the other expressed regret and the strong wish for the faculty to be reconciled. The presence of God was so palpable, there was hardly a dry eye in the room.

The Steps of Lectio Divina

As both these stories show us, if we are to draw close to the heart of God, we must be willing to listen for his still, small voice (1 Kgs 19:9–18). Luke Dysinger, O.S.B., describes lectio divina as "accepting the embrace of God."[4]

So, how does one begin? There are four simple steps. Before you begin, take time to relax into grace. Settle into the silence. Take time to grow quiet in prayer, perhaps by using the Jesus Prayer (see page 112) or by saying the Hail Mary. Take deep breaths and allow your heart to settle into a deep calm.

1. *Lectio: Take up and read.* Select a passage of scripture to read slowly. You may want to read it several times, each time a little more slowly and with longer pauses between lines and phrases, enabling the meaning to sink deep into the soul. Usually, most people read each passage at least twice.

    Consciously slow your reading. The speed with which we read newspapers or articles on the internet is not appropriate for lectio divina. One of the best ways to slow yourself down is to quietly read the passage aloud. Some people feel uncomfortable reading aloud, but give it a try. If you still feel uncomfortable reading aloud, just repeat the words slightly under your breath. Mouth the words, and vocalize just under your breath. Read each word slowly. Savor it. Let the feeling of the scripture get inside you.

2. *Meditatio: Ponder, ruminate, and meditate.* Meditation pulls the latch of the truth and looks into every closet and every cupboard. It labors to affect the heart. When a phrase resonates as we are reading, we "ruminate" on it, just like an animal chewing its cud. We ponder it with the heart.

    As the nineteenth-century contemplative minister Alexander MacLaren put it, "The commonplaces of religion are the most important. Everybody needs air, light, bread, and water. Meditate, then, upon the things most surely believed, and ever meditate until the dry stick of the commonplace truth puts forth buds and blossoms like Aaron's rod. . . . This great truth will shine into our gloom like a star into a dungeon."[5]

3. *Oratio*: *Pray*. Take time to converse with God on the themes of the reading. Talk to him friend-to-friend, as will be described in the next chapter, "The Joy of Conversing with God as a Friend."

4. *Contemplatio: Deepen your contemplation.* When you come to such a word or phrase that touches you, repeat it several times slowly. After you have savored and repeated the word or phrase, rest in stillness as long as it seems right to you.

    This resting is a wordless basking in the presence of the One who loves us without measure. Your heart will instinctively apply the word or phrase to your life. When you come to a phrase or word that touches you, repeat it over and over again very slowly; it will take on a kind of anointing.

    For instance, if you are reading Psalm 23, "The LORD is my shepherd, I shall not want. . . . He restores my soul," (NRSV:CE) the phrase "restores my soul" may seem particularly significant, something to savor. Just repeat that over and over, as long as the grace of the moment lasts.

    When you are ready, close your Bible and close your eyes. A phrase or a word may so inspire you that you offer a prayer to God, and then perhaps hear his wordless "still, small voice." Don't worry about having the "right" words to offer God. It is in the silence that we allow God to do what he wants, which is simply to love us. This is a wordless prayer, a resting, a stillness. Such prayer is a gift of God and an invitation to let God amaze you with his intimacy. Anyone who has been in love knows that there are moments of wordless communion when hearts seem as one.

Lectio divina may seem complicated, but it really isn't. The four parts don't necessarily come in set stages. For instance, you might feel an inspiration to offer a prayer early in the reading; if you do, stop and pray. You may feel yourself drawn to repeat a word or phrase and ruminate over it. You may be drawn into the loving stillness of contemplation at any moment. If you do, stop and rest silently in God's presence. You will know when it is time to begin reading the passage again.[6]

Now, let's take a moment to practice this exercise with the following scripture.

Pause in Wonder: A Moment with God

SCRIPTURE

> How sweet are your words to my taste,
> sweeter than honey to my mouth!
> Through your precepts I get understanding;
> therefore I hate every false way.
>
> Your word is a lamp to my feet
> and a light to my path.
> I have sworn an oath and confirmed it,
> to observe your righteous ordinances.
> (Ps 119:103–6, NRSV:CE)

PRAYER

Dear Lord, at times my heart is gloomy and afraid. There are times I stumble and can't find my way. Take my hand, then, and calmly lead me. May your words still me. May your scriptures embrace me, reassure me, and set my heart to dancing with joy. For your Word is a lamp to my feet, a tender embrace for my heart, a pathway for body and soul that brightens everything around me. Amen.

REFLECTION

The Word God uttered from all eternity broke into this world in the Incarnation. The words of scripture point to that eternal Word. Through and in the lines of scripture, God whispers to us, "Come close, so very close." Listen with head and heart to scripture, and you can hear the very heartbeat of God. Scripture helps us make our way through the passages of life and is the honey of our souls, because scripture reveals the One who inspired scripture and allows his breath to sync with our breath.

Starters for Journaling or Meditation

- When do you most like to read scripture? What are some of your favorite passages that you like to ponder over and over? Write or meditate upon them here.

- Remember a time scripture reading brought you calm and great joy. Write or meditate about that time.

Eight

THE JOY OF CONVERSING WITH GOD AS A FRIEND

[Black Elk's] presence brought joy to youngsters: "He loves children, & when they are about they are all over him—he is kindly, gentle, with a most marvelous sense of humor."

When not reading his prayer book, which was written in Lakota, he would have a rosary in one hand and cane in the other as the children played, rode their tricycles, or rode a horse he walked for them. Come bedtime, it was customary for him to sing them to sleep with a song from the Latin mass. He also sang a church hymn in Lakota.
—MICHAEL F. STELTENKAMP, *NICHOLAS BLACK ELK*[1]

Once I heard the story of a young priest, Fr. Walter, who visited an elderly man in the hospital. When he entered the room, Fr. Walter saw that a chair had been moved to the head of the bed. He looked at the chair, then looked at the elderly man and said, "I see I am not your first visitor today."

The man responded, "Oh no. That's Jesus' chair."

"What do you mean, 'that's Jesus' chair'?" Fr. Walter polite-ly asked.

The elderly man replied, "When I was a teenager, I found it difficult to pray to a God whom I could not see. So I took the dilemma to my pastor. He suggested whenever I prayed to put out an empty chair and imagine Jesus seated in that chair and talk to him like I would a friend. I have been doing that in all the six decades since then."

Fr. Walter did not hear from the elderly man for three days, and then got a call from the man's daughter. "Dad has died," she told him. "But there was something unusual when we found him; his head was resting not on the pillow, but on the chair." He fell asleep on the lap of his Savior.

Scripture tells us we can rely on God. "Even though I walk through the valley of the shadow of death, I will fear no evil, for you are with me; your rod and your staff comfort me" (Ps 23:4). If I skinned my knee or stepped on a tack when I was a little boy, I would run to my parents. My mother would wipe away my tears with her soft, feminine hands; my father would wipe away my tears gently with his calloused electri-cian's hands. Isn't it wonderful to know that the same hands that fashioned and created the universe can one day wipe away all our tears forever?

When was the last time you put out a chair to talk with God? He is the world's greatest listener. And when we are lonely, we can tell him about it—and he often responds by sending us the gift of spiritual friendship.

The Gift of Spiritual Friendship

Few things soothe and bring peace to our hearts more than a heartfelt talk with a close friend. We feel understood, accepted, heard. Our isolation is broken and we can connect to the world on a deeper level.

So it is with God. He already knows our needs, but he wants us to have the comforting experience of his listening to us. Is there anything more joyful than a heart-to-heart with a close friend or family member, someone who loves us unconditionally?

I had special friends like that when I was studying to become a minister at Belhaven University in Jackson, Mississippi. My roommate, Paul Evans, was also studying to be a minister; he was also a talented athlete and one of the most popular young men on campus. But he made time for me, and we talked about serious things of the heart.

My life was especially lonely in the beginning of my time at Belhaven. It was my first time away from my family. One night, when the loneliness grew particularly acute and the new world of college rattled me with its many demands and stresses, I was walking back to the dorm after a religious gathering. Paul accompanied me. I heard him sigh and say, "I am being overwhelmed by school." Since I was feeling the same way, I suggested that we talk.

We decided to take a long walk through the neighborhood surrounding Belhaven. Somehow, I felt especially safe around Paul. His very posture exuded a sense of safety and acceptance. On the surface, Paul and I were different. My world was focused on the books I read rather than emotions I felt. Paul was the quintessential people person. Extroverted, athletic, and popular even in the beginning of his first year of college, he would eventually be elected president of the student body.

Taking in deep, cleansing breaths as we walked, we both poured out all our fears and struggles, including how much we missed our familiar surroundings and all the challenges of living away from parents and family. When we got back to the dorm, I suggested we pray together. We climbed up the stairs to the flat roof of the dorm, lugging our Bibles along. We each read a couple of our favorite scriptures. Mine was Matthew 11:28: "Come to me, all you that are weary and are carrying heavy burdens, and I will give you rest" (NRSV:CE). As each of us read scripture, it seemed as though a cord of light passed from my heart to his and his to mine. We decided to meet together each evening to pray and talk together. A third was present with us—Christ.

Sharing the same dorm room meant we spent more time together, but we still took special time for prayer every evening, often going to the chapel on the basement floor of our dorm. We trusted each other with the most hidden secrets of our hearts. I clearly remember the night I finally had the courage to talk about Daddy's illness and the terror it caused me growing up. He met me with acceptance. With Paul I felt an unconditional love that I hadn't experienced since my grandfather died. The only other time I had felt so loved was with a favorite high school teacher. My conversations with Paul helped me open my heart to let in the love of many others. Our times together enabled us to open wide our hearts with love and appreciation for everyone we met.

Today Paul is a married Presbyterian minister in northern Georgia and I am celibate Catholic clergyman living 150 miles away. Even so, we have kept up those healing conversations by phone and by visits. My times with Paul prepared me for the time God's love invaded me in that church in Selma. My heart was being made ready for that touch of God that eventually led me to the Catholic Church. When I started attending a Catholic parish, I had Paul's support and encouragement. I found in my friendship with Paul a healing presence for the hurts of my past and a daily joy that pierced my loneliness.

I have several spiritual friends in my life now. One that lifts me up every day is my spiritual friendship with Joanna Brunson. She and I talk daily. We talk about the highs and lows of our day, our joys and sorrows, then take turns praying for each other. We also meet together nearly weekly. Joanna; her fiancé, Martin Wolf; Deacon Robert; Joan Andros; and I gather for spiritual conversation and a celebratory meal. Joanna and I have both received a profound healing of our souls through these conversations.

Aelred of Rievaulx wrote that a joy that is shared is doubled, and in my conversational spiritual friendships with others I often see my joys double, even triple. The great reality is that we can allow God to become a soul friend, daily talking with him about our joys, our struggles, and the very stuff of our lives.

Take Time Alone with God

It is important to have sacred time alone with God, to be in his presence. This is the time to talk with him as a friend. All believers, not just deacons and priests, need to take time each day to talk to God. No matter how advanced our prayer lives may be, we still need to engage God in conversation. Conversational prayer is an intimate communication between friends. Jesus listens to us; we listen to him.

Few things comfort us more or better than someone who lovingly listens. Jesus—the greatest listener, the greatest friend—experienced our fears, stresses, and worries. He understands us more than anyone does.

I especially remember the effect conversational prayer had on Jake, a young man who attended a retreat we were leading for the teens of a parish in the Midwest. The theme of the retreat was prayer, and we explored with the teens different forms of prayer: imaginative prayer, contemplative prayer, the Rosary, as well as other ways of praying.

The pastor had told me about Jake and his family when we first arrived. They had seemed like a happy, normal family. Jake was exceptionally bright. His father's job as an accountant at a local business seemed to pay very well because they definitely lived an upscale life. The family took vacations to Italy, Greece, Thailand, and other places. His father had even given Jake a two-year-old Porsche for his sixteenth birthday, which Jake loved to show off.

That upscale life came to a screeching halt when the papers and TV loudly proclaimed that Jake's father had been arrested for embezzling more than $2 million from the company that had employed him. For several weeks the details came out in the media. Jake's mother filed for divorce. Since he had no real defense, his father pled guilty and was given a twelve-year sentence in state prison. Jake lost his car, his father's presence, and his world in one fell swoop.

During the retreat, I noticed that Jake seemed to have a hard time focusing, and sat silently during the discussion and sharing parts of the retreat. A few times his eyes grew red and teared up, but I knew it was not from something that moved him in the presentation. It was not hard to guess what that something else was.

The last session of the retreat for the teens was on conversational prayer. In closing, we prayed conversationally as a group. We thanked God, told him our needs, and prayed for others. When it came time for Jake to pray, he made a sound in his throat, then said, "I want to pray but I just can't." He collapsed into rib-shaking sobs, huffing out the words, "I no longer have a father." He continued to cry inconsolably, imploring, "Pray for me. Will you please pray for me?"

Without any prompting from Deacon Robert or me, all the teens moved as one, standing and laying hands on his head and shoulders in that ancient Christian ritual of intercession and blessing. Each of them said, "We love you, Jake. We are here for you." One by one, they prayed out confident, comforting words of conversational prayer. When they finished, they pulled him to his feet and tenderly embraced him.

Finally, Jake was able to offer a prayer of his own: "Dear Father in heaven, you are my father even when my earthly father disappears."

I later learned that Jake started counseling with the pastor of his church. The group decided to form a weekly conversational prayer group led by one of the religious sisters assigned to the parish. It was hard for Jake, but he got on track with his life knowing he had a Father in heaven as well as brothers and sisters in the other members of the prayer group.

Beginning Conversational Prayer

Conversational prayer is not new. Its roots are ancient. St. Alphonsus de Liguori, who could be called the patron saint of conversational prayer, lived in Italy during the eighteenth century. In *The Way of Conversing with God as a Friend,* published in 1752, Liguori wrote: "God's heart has no greater concern than to love us and to make itself loved by us." This is the core principle of conversational prayer. Liguori adds, "Always act toward God like faithful friends who consult with each other on everything. . . . Accustom yourself to speak to God, one-to-one, in a familiar manner as to the dearest friend you have and who loves you best of all."[2]

Not only do we speak with God in conversational prayer; God speaks to us. St. Alphonsus writes: "God will not make himself heard by you in a voice that reaches your ears but rather in a voice that only your heart knows well."[3]

Any prayer in which you converse personally with God can be called "conversational prayer." Rosalind Rinker, a former Protestant missionary to China, has written many books on conversational prayer and has led hundreds of workshops on the subject. She worked closely with the Catholic bishop of Little Rock in teaching conversational prayer throughout the diocese; this work influenced the widely used Little Rock Bible Study.

Like St. Alphonsus Liguori, Rinker defines conversational prayer as a form of "spontaneous, childlike prayer, put out from hearts directly to the heart of Jesus." As much as possible, she urges people to pray out loud as they converse with God. I have found that forming the words with my mouth and vocalizing them just under my breath physically reinforces the prayer just as well. Other people write out their conversational prayers in a special notebook or journal.

Four Steps to Conversational Prayer

The following steps of prayer are drawn from the Catholic tradition and scripture.

1. *Lord, you are here.* Recognize the Lord's nearness. Welcome him out loud or silently in your own words. I often pray: "You are so near me, Lord, closer to me than my breath. Please open your listening heart to my prayers."

2. *Thank you, Lord.* Think over all the ways Jesus has loved and cared for you. Name some of those times, and thank him for them. Offer praise, worship, and adoration.

3. *Come near me and help me, Lord.* Take your needs to Jesus one by one. Tell him about your cares, admit your sins, and ask him for guidance.

4. *I pray for my brothers and sisters, the entire Church, and the whole of creation.* In this final step, begin to move beyond your own personal needs and to pray for others, thinking of their needs and cares. Pray for this hurting world of ours.

Pause in Wonder: A Moment with God

SCRIPTURE

Let your gentleness be known to everyone. The Lord is near. Do not worry about anything, but in everything by prayer and supplication with thanksgiving let your requests be made known to God. And the peace of God, which surpasses all understanding, will guard your hearts and your minds in Christ Jesus. (Phil 4:5–7, NRSV:CE)

PRAYER

> God, in my busyness,
> in the intensity of my living and my work,
> I have forgotten many of the times
> you have fanned me with your very breath,
> the times you have comforted me,
> letting me sink into your cushioning embrace,
> the times the touch of your hand has sent warmth
>   through me,
> the times you have shown me a glistening horizon,
> the times you have blessed me with hallowed
>   mystery.

Dear Lord, you love each of us as if we were the only one you had to love. Give me the grace to talk to you one-to-one as with a most familiar friend. You are indeed the greatest listener. Guide me to speak to you so my heart can beat in rhythm with your sacred heart. Amen.

REFLECTION

Imagine Jesus is seated in a chair facing you. You see the light of heaven that surrounds him. Let the deep stillness of his presence enter your heart. First, thank him for all the ways his love has helped you. Next, tell him your needs. Tell him about the ways you need his help in your life. Now, tell him about other people and situations that need his help. Pray for peace and justice. Pray that human life be respected and protected from the moment of conception until the moment of natural death. See the whole world surrounded and embraced by the light of Christ, which streams from his body. Gently return to this time and rest in the stillness.

———————

Fear leaves all of us with an intense sense of powerlessness and vulnerability. When we are overcome by fear, Harvard Medical School psychiatrist Edward M. Hallowell says, "Don't wring your hands, clasp them. . . . Prayer or meditation can change the state of your brain."[4] Talk to God when you feel worried or fearful. Jesus listens to us; we listen to him. Hardly anything comforts and eases us more than someone who lovingly listens. Jesus—the greatest listener, the greatest friend—experienced our fears, our stresses, and our worries. He understands us more than anyone. He grasps our hand.

In the next chapter, I've asked Robert to share with you from his own experiences of encountering God in prayer, particularly contemplative prayer. As he shares his story, let the Spirit speak to your heart and show you how you, too, can draw closer to him in your daily prayer encounters.

Starters for Journaling or Meditation

Writing out our prayers is a way of making our prayer real
and concrete. Write out and compose the following prayer by
filling in the blanks. When you finish the prayer, recite it as
the prayer of your heart.

> Dear God, today I thank you for . . .
>
> Have mercy on these people for whom I have
> promised to pray . . .
>
> Please take these worries from me . . .
>
> Jesus, I want to share with you what is going on in
> my life . . .
>
> Thank you for all these ways you have shown your
> love to me this week . . .
>
> Help me to love and serve you better. Quiet my
> heart, so I can hear you speak. Thank you for
> always remaining near to me. Amen.

Nine

FINDING JOY IN CONTEMPLATIVE PRAYER

BY DEACON ROBERT HERRMANN

"Every morning, (Kateri) even in the bitterest winter, she stood before the chapel door until it opened at four and remained there until after the last Mass. Out from her Caughnawaga cabin at dawn and straight-way to chapel to adore the Blessed Sacrament, hear every Mass; back again during the day to hear instruction, and at night for a last prayer or Benediction."

—FR. LAWRENCE LOVASIK, S.V.D., *BLESSED KATERI TEKAKWITHA*[1]

I was sixteen when I began to feel something was missing in my life. At the time I was keeping busy with school, work, and dating; in my spare time I was turning an old Volkswagen into a hot rod and cycling a couple of hundred miles a week. And yet, all these things that occupied my time left me flat. I ached for much more out of life. I needed much more.

Around this time, I saw a newspaper article by Reverend Billy Graham. I remember how lovingly he spoke about God and God's desire to love us. Though I was Catholic, I began to read his articles nearly every day. At the end of his articles, he always urged his readers, "If you have a church, go to it; if you don't, find one."

That impressed me, and I started going to Mass again—I had been refusing to go with my parents for a couple of years. This time Mass didn't bore me. It garnered my rapt attention. I got to know two Sisters of Mercy, Sr. Amalia and Sr. Alice. I remember their beaming expressions and glowing cheeks. They were both full of fun and laughter. Sure, they were nuns, yet they were real, down-to-earth, and bursting with kindness. They enjoyed life to its fullest. Sr. Alice, who taught third grade, used to have a banner in her classroom that read: "The fact that silence is golden probably explains why there is so little of it!"

Something lit up both their personalities. I soon began to realize that that something was related to prayer. They both spent over an hour a day in private prayer in addition to going to Mass and praying with the sick and homebound of our parish. I wanted what they had, and I figured that what I needed would come through learning to pray every day, like they did.

I started getting up early each morning to pray in the only way I knew: I said all the prayers I'd learned in childhood, except those I'd learned to say in my mother's native tongue, German. (I'd forgotten all my German due to lack of use.) Every morning I would go through the same routine of spoken prayers. At first this was satisfying and fulfilling enough, but soon I would begin to feel a sense that I needed something to touch and explore.

At the end of one of my short prayer times, I asked God, "What's missing? What am I not getting? I know I'm supposed to pray longer, but I don't know what to do. God, please help me." God must have noticed my frustration, and in a few moments the words from deep inside me bubbled up, "Why don't you just be quiet?"

When I heard those words, I felt a rush of understanding. *Just be still.* Words are not necessary to be with God. I began taking large, deep, savoring breaths, keenly aware of my own heartbeat. I was flooded with warmth.

During this time, I also began to read the Bible and other spiritual writings. Inspiration from those wise and greathearted people who had gone before me sped me along my journey. I read about a playful St. Francis who met God as a very young man in the wonder of creation and in the poor. I was inspired by the lives of Martin Luther King Jr., who gave his life for peace and justice, and Jose Sandoval, who was martyred at age fourteen because of his love of God. I reveled in the wit and wisdom of Teresa of Avila and so many others. Reading spiritual books entranced me more than a page-turning adventure novel.

In short, through that quiet, through Sr. Amalia and Sr. Alice, and through reading the Bible and other spiritual works, I found myself in the middle of an adventure—the gladness of loving God and all that God loves. In short, I was discovering the immense joy of contemplative prayer.

Sharing the Joy in Contemplative Prayer

Contemplative prayer is not something we achieve by hard work but is simply surrendering, allowing God to go into the interior of our being in order to love us. In contemplative prayer, we rest in God's unearned love. We taste God's glory, and the light of that glory begins to shine through the whole of our personality. Contemplation is less like climbing a ladder, and more like taking a sunbath in God's love, a sunbath that fills us wondrously and leads to abiding joy.

In his book *Pensées*, Blaise Pascal observed that every human being has a craving for God. "This he tries to fill in vain with everything around him, seeking in things that are not there the help he cannot find . . . since this infinite abyss can be filled only with . . . God himself."[2] As I continued to seek God in prayer, I yearned for my soul to be invaded by the Lord. I wanted the blank spots to be filled with God's love. I discovered that spirituality and prayer are not so much about running an obstacle course successfully as they are about being open to grace—the love of God reaching down to us and elevating us into his joy. It is not about being a spiritual competitor, but about holding out a cup for God to fill.

It is so easy to fall into a view of prayer and spirituality that would make us think that anything we gain from prayer or reflection is the result of our own hard work. Spirituality and prayer are about letting God do what he wants to do most, which is simply to love us and share his bliss with us in creation. God is a tremendous lover. His love is the ground of the cosmos, all creation, and our very selves. He loves us body and soul, down to the very cells of our fingernails. He looks down on us with a smile that the whole cosmos cannot contain and yearns for us to smile back. He wants us to say yes to that love and, through his grace, love him in return, and love all that he loves. This love can excite us and cause us to exult in God and the creation God sustains. It is an ecstasy that God's enormous love became touchable, real, down-to-earth, everyday love in Jesus; it remains physical and tangible in the Eucharist where we taste his love and join in a limitless rejoicing that can, if we let it, transfigure us. In prayer, we take the whole of our lives and let God soak it with the wonder of his caring.

Anchoring Our Hearts in the Stillness

One way to anchor our hearts in God's stillness is to softly repeat short prayers such as the Jesus Prayer or litanies. Such prayers center our hearts in the silence. The Rosary can also be a powerful way to dispose ourselves to the joy of contemplative prayer.

The Rosary has spawned many saints, and I have witnessed the benefits of using this form of prayer as a way to prepare for extended periods of resting in God. To use the Rosary this way, it is essential to slow it down, repeating each prayer slowly with devotion as though whispering into the ear of the Beloved.

Much of what we say in this section on the Jesus Prayer can also apply to the Rosary and to litanies like the Litany of the Most Precious Blood.

The Jesus Prayer

The Jesus Prayer, based on an early Christian prayer practice, can warm your heart and ease you and brighten you with immense joy. It has a long tradition in the Eastern Catholic and Eastern Orthodox traditions. It involves slowly and tenderly repeating the name of our Savior, Jesus. Some Western spiritual leaders such as St. Bernard of Clairvaux also had a devotion to the invocation of the name of Jesus. Read the following quote from him on the Jesus prayer. Read it slowly and perhaps several times:

Write what you will, I shall not relish it unless it
tells of Jesus. . . . Jesus to me is honey in the mouth,
music in the ear, a song in the heart.

Again, it is a medicine. Does one of us feel sad?
Let the name of Jesus come into his heart and from
there spring to his mouth, so that shining like the
dawn it may dispel all darkness. . . . Does someone
fall into sin? Does his despair even urge him to
suicide? Let him but invoke this life-giving name
and his will to live will at once be renewed.[3]

Are you experiencing a need for simple peace, for healing for
the sense that your prayers are being heard? Are you in need
of the merciful hand of God? Call out now upon his Son, the
Word of God Incarnate. Say it now, and repeat it often: "Lord
Jesus, have mercy on me."

The most famous book on the Jesus Prayer is *The Way of
the Pilgrim*, a spiritual classic written by an anonymous Russian
peasant who yearned to find out what the apostle Paul meant
when he urged people to "pray without ceasing" (1 Thes 5:17).
A *starets*, or spiritual adviser and monastic elder, learned of the
peasant's desire for understanding and taught him the Jesus
Prayer, urging the peasant to pray this prayer frequently during
the day.

As the pilgrim prayed, a fiery flame of tender joy burned
in his heart. The prayer descended from his head to his heart,
becoming a "prayer of the heart." He also carried a Bible with
him and read a gospel every day. The prayer transfigured the
created world around him. The invocation of the name of
Jesus gladdened his way.

He bursts with delight when he writes:

When I prayed in my heart, everything around
me seemed delightful and marvelous. The trees,

> the grass, the birds, the air, the light seemed to be telling me that they existed for man's sake, that they witnessed to the love of God for man, that all things prayed to God and sang his praise.

The Jesus Prayer not only lifted the pilgrim's burdens; it transformed his relations with his fellow human beings. He writes:

> Again I started off on my wanderings. But now I did not walk along as before, filled with care. The invocation of the Name of Jesus gladdened my way. Everybody was kind to me. If anyone harms me I have only to think, "How sweet is the Prayer of Jesus!" and the injury and the anger alike pass away and I forget it all.[4]

Through the centuries, stressed-out Christians have turned to prayers such as the Jesus Prayer to ease them into stillness. The exact wording of the prayer is not as important as the intention behind it. Orthodox Christians, who have a long history of praying the Jesus Prayer, use a variety of forms. Eastern Christians view any invocation of the holy name of Jesus as an authentic Jesus Prayer. Over the years the prayer crystallized into the phrase, "Lord Jesus Christ, Son of the Living God, have mercy on me, a sinner."

However, the Jesus Prayer and similar prayers, in themselves, are not recited simply as a means to attain stress relief. Rather, the prayer invites God into the far reaches of the soul. This is what calms us, stills us, and ultimately delights us as it did the pilgrim. God loves every one of us as if we were the only one he had to love. We are his joy.

How to Pray the Jesus Prayer

The simplest forms of the prayer usually work best. The earliest form of the prayer was simply to repeat lovingly the name *Jesus* over and over again. Many people simply pray, "Jesus, Lord Jesus."

Most people offer the prayer while seated. Find a chair that is not too hard, otherwise you will fidget with discomfort. Use a chair that is soft, but at the same time supports your back in an upright position. Some use the shorter version of the prayer as I do. Deacon Eddie, forever the person of tradition, uses the classic full prayer, "Lord Jesus Christ, Son of the Living God, have mercy on me, a sinner."

Start by surrendering to God. Begin your time of prayer by first abandoning yourself and your prayer time into God's care. Ask him to take charge. Perhaps say a prayer like this: "Lord, I turn this prayer time over to you. Do with me what you will." Others prefer the scriptural prayer: "Father, into your hands I commend my spirit" (Lk 23:46). After you have surrendered your prayer time into God's hands, begin softly saying your Jesus Prayer. Say it out loud, if possible; or if not, at least pray it under your breath.

When Your Thoughts Wander

We all have busy attics. Wandering thoughts are part of being human. I'm sure Jesus had wandering thoughts when he prayed; he was human, after all. Wandering thoughts in prayer are not sinful; they are natural. You didn't will to have these thoughts; they came unbidden. Wandering thoughts in prayer can be a symptom of pent-up stress; the thoughts were with us all along, suppressed, pushed down, and locked inside.

Think of what happens when a capped bottle of cola is shaken. The bottled-up fizz creates great pressure inside the bottle. Finally, when the cap is taken off, the fizz spews out the top, relieving the pressure. Our busyness and preoccupations cap the thoughts within us. When we take time for the Jesus Prayer, we take the cap off and the thoughts, which were with us all along but hidden, emerge into our consciousness. Gently turn your thoughts back to prayer. Don't add to your stress by becoming angry with yourself. After all, the last act of your will before a random thought emerged was an act of loving God, saying the Jesus Prayer. You didn't choose this distraction. Rather, you surrendered yourself to God for the length of your prayer time. What happens in that prayer time is God's business.

When a wandering thought interrupts your Jesus Prayer, the best way to handle it is simply to notice it, then let it pass by. Next, return to saying your Jesus Prayer. Don't focus on the thought. Think of a wandering thought as a bird that flies by in the air; you notice it and let it fly away, but you don't make a nest for it. If it helps you focus, you can physically say the prayer with an Eastern Catholic rosary, a prayer cord that contains a hundred knots you finger each time you say the Jesus Prayer.

If, in the course of a thirty-minute prayer time, wandering thoughts interrupt your prayer a hundred times and you return to saying your prayer each time, you have made a hundred separate acts of loving God.

After you finish saying your Jesus Prayer, rest in the love of God. More than anything else God simply wants to love us. Let your heart sink into the ease of silent adoration.

Pause in Wonder: A Moment with God

SCRIPTURE

> O LORD, my heart is not lifted up,
> my eyes are not raised too high;
> I do not occupy myself with things
> too great and too marvelous for me.
> But I have calmed and quieted my soul,
> like a weaned child with its mother;
> my soul is like the weaned child that is with me.
>
> O Israel, hope in the LORD
> from this time on and for evermore.
> (Ps 131, NRSV:CE)

PRAYER

Dear Lord, may your holy name ever be on my tongue, warm my heart, and quiet my mind, for the name of Jesus holds more power than the entire universe. In your name are comfort, consolation, peace, and stillness. The name of Jesus calms our storms, smooths our pathways, brightens our lives, and stills our hearts. Amen.

REFLECTION

Hiding from others, God, and ourselves expends a great deal of emotional and physical energy and leaves us strained and tired. When we take time to notice and acknowledge our emotions, or how our bodies feel at the moment—when we are honest—the energy we have tied up in repression can be redirected for more effective living and loving. Our whole being loosens up and relaxes. We are freed to be more present to the here and now. So many of the authors of scripture had that honest awareness of themselves. When we acknowledge where we are at the moment, it's easier for God's love to penetrate us more deeply.

Starters for Journaling or Meditation

- Write about a time when a burden you were carrying inside lightened because of prayer.

- What do you think it means to lovingly rest in God?

- Has there ever been a time when prayer has so calmed you that it was easier to make prudential decisions? Write or meditate about that time.

- What do you think the concept that prayer can brighten our lives with joy means?

Ten

FINDING JOY IN COMPASSION

The heart that is inflamed in this way embraces
the entire creation—man, birds, animals.... At the
recollection of them, and at the sight of them, such
a man's eyes fill with tears that arise from the great
compassion which presses on his heart.
                              —ISAAC OF NINEVEH[1]

When our hearts open to wonder and joy, it is not a solitary
experience; we want to reach out to others and put them in
touch with God, the true source of all healing, joy, and wonder. The touch of God in our lives should lead us to develop a
devout compassion for our fellow humans who hurt and for
a hurting creation.

In the gospels, we read many times that Jesus was moved
with compassion for each individual or group he healed or for
whom he worked wonders (see Mt 9:36; Mk 1:41). The central
trait of Jesus that infuses the gospels is his compassion: He was
moved with compassion for the crowds who were like sheep
without a shepherd (see Mt 9:36). He showed compassion to
a leper (see Mk 1:41), to the two blind men (see Mt 20:34),

and to the widow of Nain (see Lk 7:13) as well as to many he met during his ministry.

The compassion of Jesus is his response to the rejected, the poor, and the struggling, whom people so easily ignore others. In his paper "From Intimacy to Compassion," Eduardo Aguero writes,

> In Mt 14:13–21, after he was informed of John's beheading, Jesus decides to cross the lake and retire to the desert to be alone with his Father. It is in the same desert of his sorrow and intimacy with the Father that he experiences compassion for the crowd that caught up with him. Here contemplation and action meet. His compassion is translated into healing and feeding the people.[2]

As we continue to experience joy and wonder in these encounters with God, these moments of contemplation bear fruit in our lives to the degree that our boundless joy inspires us to invite others to the eucharistic banquet, to feed those who are in touch with their hunger and thirst for God.

The Compassionate Christ

In his emptying of himself, Jesus revealed the very heart of God and showed that God's fatherhood is revealed most fully in his loving compassion. God shows himself most fully not in his might but in tenderness and kindheartedness. As the Word Incarnate, Jesus showed his divinity not in great majesty but in his capacity to care for us as our own brother.

That Jesus shared our human poverty in order that we may share his divine richness is the summit of New Testament teaching, the apex of our hope. His stooping, the infinite breadth of his mercy, and his self-giving appeals to the deepest feelings of the heart. "For the Son of Man did not come to be served but to serve and to give his life as a ransom for many" (Mk 10.45).

It is only when we look to that Lord in his tenderhearted-ness, and see there the very lowest point to which he stooped, the Cross, that we will be drawn to yield our deep sensing, feelings, and lives to him. We should pattern our lives on him and empty ourselves out in compassion for our sisters and brothers, our very earth, and the cosmos that was brought forth by the touch of his breath.

Jesus came down to our level to raise us up to his. He expe-rienced the things we experience, lived the human life that we live. His self-emptying compassion made us shareholders in the boundless joy of his immortal life. The eternal wonder of the gift of his very self means that if we are to live for anything nobler than the fleeting self-aggrandizement of the ego, we too must learn to stoop to forgive, to impart ourselves and our very lives to others in bigheartedness.

If we are ever to feel pure joy and communicate that joy to others, we need to imitate Jesus in his compassion. He has loved us and given himself for us. He has set us an example that he commends to us by his own word when he tells us that if a grain of wheat is to bring forth much fruit, it must die, else it abides alone. Unless we die, we never truly live; unless we die to ourselves in compassion for others, and hand in hand with Jesus, we live alone in the solitude of a self-enclosed self-regard (see Jn 12:24).

The gospels portray the whole of Christ's life as a rev-elation of God's compassion, particularly Jesus' parable of the prodigal son, whose father never abandoned his son no matter how far he wandered from his father's loving care. We see God's loving compassion for us and the whole of creation reach its highest, most eloquent expression in the passion and crucifixion of Christ.

Experiencing God's Compassion

One of the keys to having compassion for others is being able to acknowledge with gratitude the compassion God has given us and calls us to give ourselves. We are like the prodigal son, who instead of a harsh reprimand receives the unrestrained mercy of the father and a joyous celebration upon returning.

How have you experienced this to be true in your own life? As you contemplate your life, do any stories come to mind that illustrate the kindness and compassion of God, who walked with you during the lowest moments of your life? If we deny and soft-pedal our own history of hurt, we will keep our distance from others and our distance from God.

If we are to become compassionate, we must open our hearts to allow God to mend and heal these broken places. When we deny our losses and need, we push them way down, deep inside, where we wall them off from the rest of ourselves, and our personalities can turn toxic. But if we allow God to show us these hidden wounds and grieve our losses, God will guide us through (not around) the valley of the shadow of death.

The Sweat Lodge

Despite the diversity and complexity of the cultures and religions around the world, as human beings we share one thing in common: our most important truths and spiritual realities are found not in abstractions, but through stories, real-life examples. And so, it is through stories and imagery that we most readily grasp compassion. In my case, as a

Native American Christian, some of my most profound prayer encounters with God have taken place in an American Indian sweat lodge.

Does this surprise you? One of the beautiful things about the Church has been her global reach and her ability to spread the message of God's love using the symbols and cultural insights of peoples throughout the world in her missionary work. Pope St. John Paul II encouraged Native Americans to keep the cultural ways as long as they did not contradict the teachings of Christ:

> It is time to think of the present and of the future. Today, people are realizing more and more clearly that we all belong to the one human family, and are meant to walk and work together in mutual respect, understanding, trust and love. Within this family *each people preserves and expresses its own identity and enriches others with its gifts of culture,* tradition, customs, stories, song, dance, art and skills.
>
> From the very beginning, the Creator bestowed his gifts on each people. It is clear that stereotyping, prejudice, bigotry and racism demean the human dignity which comes from the hand of the Creator and which is seen in variety and diversity. I encourage you, as native people belonging to the different tribes and nations in the East, South, West, and North, *to preserve and keep alive your cultures, your languages, the values and customs* which have served you well in the past and which provide a solid foundation for the future. . . .
>
> Your gifts can also be expressed even more fully in the Christian way of life. *The Gospel of Jesus Christ is at home in every people. It enriches, uplifts, and purifies every culture.*[3]

This greatly encouraged me to include my culture in my spiritual journey, the culture I learned from my father and my grandfather, who were both Native Americans and baptized Christians.

The sweat lodge is one expression of that culture. It is a hut with a pit in the center for hot stones. At nighttime, a fire would be lit, and stones put in the fire. We would gather in a circle around the stones in the pits, say prayers together, and smoke a pipe that symbolized peace.

My Native friends, Jerome Inness and Claire Dakota Inness, held a sweat lodge every month or so on their land in Standing Rock, Alabama, about an hour and a half from my home in Columbus, Georgia. The event was for people of Native American descent, but some other seekers also joined us. All day long participants helped to build the lodge. Due to my disability, I couldn't help building, but I sat and engaged in conversation while the sweat lodge was constructed.

When the stones were hot, we gathered in a circle close to the fire in the lodge, sweating out the toxins of our body while the Holy Spirit was cleansing us from within. It was a profound way of praying, penitential and yet joyful at the same time. As I sat with my bare legs against the earthen floor, I thought of God's gift of the earth that sustained me and how it reminded me of his sustaining love and sustaining power. I came from this earth. I would return to this earth. Yet I also came from the mystery that envelops this earth in God's embrace as lover of the beloved. Some people would pour water on the stones and blast the whole lodge full of steam. It reminded me of incense in church and prayers lifting to God.

Throughout the night, people would move in and out of the lodge, cooling down and continuing to share their joys and sorrows as we passed a talking stick. As it was passed around the circle, each person said a prayer, told a story, quoted scripture, or shared some meaningful event. One person started by saying, "O sacred and mysterious one, we send up a voice. Come be with us, manifest yourself in our heart. Show us that we are all related." I felt the tenderness of our Lord in my heart as we prayed. I felt connected with each person in that lodge, the connectedness of the Church, the connectedness of all humanity.

Shortly after this, I went back into the sweat lodge and received a vision. I saw Christ standing beside a stream in the Smoky Mountains. Crystal-clear water rolled and gurgled over the stones. I saw Christ clothed and vested in deerskin; he had his hands opened and raised up in prayer and healing. From the openness between his arms, *nowhetee* (healing or medicine) came from his open hands. As he did that, I felt a wind blow over me that I knew to be the wind of the Spirit.

I then saw the animals of the forest gather around this Christ, who had his arms wide open in healing and blessing. I saw torn and hurt animals made well and bounding off, back into the woods. Then, as I stood next to him on the rock, I noticed that there were also people surrounding him. I saw a deer wounded by an arrow, his face drawn in terror, and beside the deer I saw a three-year-old who had no one to love him and the look of dejection on his face. In that moment, I recognized myself as that young, sad child. I recalled the time Daddy was in the midst of some of his delusions and threatened to kill me and slice me up with a knife. I remembered the terror of that and saw the stark fear on my young face in the vision.

At that moment, Christ turned toward me, lifting his arms in blessing and healing. As the healing flowed, I saw the face of the rejected child soften and relax. I felt in my heart that

God was loving me and healing my past pain. He continued to heal others, too—in the vision, I saw a widow who had just lost her husband. Christ walked out to her and embraced her, saying, "Your husband may be gone for a while, but I can embrace you in his absence."

I talked about my emerging vision with the people in the lodge. As I watched the vision, I saw the healing growing dim. I cried out, "O Great One, O Gentle One clothed in deerskin, why is the healing dimming?"

I heard these words in response, "I do not choose to heal alone. I do not choose to work my medicine alone, but I call all of you to work with me. May your hands and feet connect with the world and with me so that you may be a conduit of the world's greatest mercy. . . . Join with me in your hearts, making a circle of hands. In the inner part of the circle, bless and pray for those who are wounded. Let the wounded stand in the center of your circle, those wounded in heart, wounded in body, wounded spiritually, wounded by not yet knowing my love."

As I lifted up my arms and the others lifted up their arms, I saw the healed deer scampering out into the woods. I saw children filled with pain and loneliness grow still and be peaceful. As the grace of healing that I received from Christ poured out from my heart, I could feel the pain of those in front of me. Healing was a connection that ran both ways. As the healing diminished again, I heard Jesus say, "Let me bring to you some helpers in healing."

I then saw those that loved me: my parents (even though we had hard times, they truly loved me); my grandparents; my Aunt Genella; and Margaret Cox, one of my favorite teachers. All stood beside me. The strength that they had given me, the mystery they implanted within me, was part of how healing would come.

Weapons of Compassion

The vision grew dimmer, and I heard Christ speaking again, "Now I will show you the hardest part of healing: the changing of weapons."

The message puzzled me. "The changing of weapons"— what did this mean? Then in an instant I was standing there at the river and was yet in a totally different place in the way that such things can happen only in dreams and visions. The medicine that radiated from Christ carried me to a different place. I stood before a tree that reached high into the sky, towering so tall that I could not see the top of it. I stood in awe of the tree, and the image and the symbol of the tree became clear to me. I thought of that great tree of peace that St. Bonaventure spoke of in his visionary meditation, "The Tree of Life" (*Lignum Vitae*). His vast tree, he wrote, symbolized Christ, who came from the stump of Jesse. I thought of the Native symbol of the tree, the great tree of peace in the Native prophet and peacemaker Deganawida's vision.[4]

Christ said to me, "I will teach you the lesson of the changing of weapons." He then reached inside me, to that place where we feel our feelings, and drew out of me a weapon, a stone war club. Christ said, "Inside, you hold many weapons. When you were a child, so much frightened you. The other face of fear is bitterness, the bitterness of weapons that would strike back, that would hurt others. Now reach in yourself and pull out the weapons."

I reached inside my heart and took out all sorts of knives and war clubs and arrows that came from me—the products of my hurt, the children of my fear, the weapons I used to

strike back and hold off the fear. I drew them out of my vitals
and placed them under the roots of the great tree, where they
were transformed into farming tools to work for healing and
peace. As the prophet Isaiah wrote:

> He shall judge between the nations,
> and set terms for many peoples.
> They shall beat their swords into plowshares
> and their spears into pruning hooks;
> One nation shall not raise the sword against
>   another,
> nor shall they train for war again. (Is 2:4)

As I stood on the rock with Christ, I saw a row of people in
front of me with familiar faces. These were the people who had
hurt me, the people toward whom I held both unfelt and felt
anger: a teacher who had made fun of me, students who had
laughed at me when I was growing up, and the people I would
avoid if I saw them in a mall. All of them appeared before me
now. My eyes wanted to turn away; I had held such weapons
of harshness in me. I tried to let my heart reach out to them
and let the healing rays flow from me. My limbs weakened
and wavered as I looked at all the people of my pain. I could
not look them in the eye.

I saw not only the people who had hurt me but also the
people I had hurt. I saw that I too had inflicted wounds.
I could look at them and see and feel what my words and
actions had done to them. Visible in their faces were the scars
of my withdrawing myself from them and saying hard things
to them. I could feel it all, and I collapsed inside. I spoke out
with the language of my heart, standing near Christ, who
stood beside me: "I cannot do this by myself. I cannot go
through this alone. I can do this only with your help."

Then I heard Christ say in the heart's wordless communion: "These are your greatest teachers, these people of your pain. These are your teachers in becoming a healer." I stretched out my hands. I could look them in the face now, and the healing again flowed not only to them but also to the whole multitude.

My mind and my heart came back to the sweat lodge. I sat there on the ground, which was now moist with my sweat. Sweat poured down until my eyes burned with the salt. Tears streamed from my eyes. Stillness like eternity filled the lodge. I then told the others of my vision, which is really the vision of all of us. It is the vision that in some way every one of us has, if we will but stop a moment and see it. I said to the group, "Let us now in silence all go to the root of the tree of life and begin changing our weapons into medicine, for we are all called to be healers, and this is the pathway of healers." After a long silence, we exited the lodge, letting the jolt of the freezing wind cool our heated, near-naked bodies. The wind quickly cooled us, and a sparkling joy showed itself in all our features.

We gathered near the fire to warm from the cool. We then entered the lodge for another round. A few people prayed; some chanted. I sat in silence, and in the silence, without words, I heard Christ's message.

> You cannot be healed without becoming a healer. Gather in all the love that you have known—the love of all those whose gaze became my gaze—all the touches, all the love that met you in creation. The ways of healing are the ways of touching and being touched, feeling the pain in some way as I feel it. I heal by inhabiting the deepest places of the deepest hurts.
>
> My healing is my calling, my calling to join in the healing of earth and sky. Join me, all of you.

> Join me in the mending. I am the healer who loves
> and heals through many healers and the lover who
> loves through many who love. . . . Look in the eyes
> of the people of your pain. I am the one who ties
> together that which has been torn and mends that
> which has been ripped and wounded.

The world changed for a moment, caught up in an eternity of light. It sparkled, and I dwelled in the eternity of its sparkling. After this vision, each of us exited the lodge, returned to the old farmhouse for a jubilant, festive potluck meal, and began our journey home. Fully entered into, compassion can be a source of unutterable joy. Jesus' compassion in his death and torture gave way to the central symbol and reality of joy: his resurrection and with it the resurrection of the world, the new creation, the New Jerusalem.

Pause in Wonder: A Moment with God

Scripture

As God's chosen ones, holy and beloved, clothe yourselves with compassion, kindness, humility, meekness, and patience. Bear with one another and, if anyone has a complaint against another, forgive each other; just as the Lord has forgiven you, so you also must forgive. (Col 3:12–13, NRSV:CE)

Prayer

Dear Lord, you have shown your immense compassion to us in your consolation and in your mercy. In the sacraments your kindness touches us, embraces us in tangible ways, and calls to us to let our words and actions toward others become sacraments of your presence. Keep me always close to your heart and by showing compassion, help me to bring others into your heart. Amen.

Reflection

Since God's love flows over with compassion, compassion flows unstoppably from the center of his heart. It is in his nature to be kind. And when we open up our hearts to that compassion, it trains our hearts to act in kind ways, letting our hearts overflow to others with the same compassion God shows us.

Starters for Journaling or Meditation

- God uses our human experiences—such as the sweat lodge experience of Deacon Eddie's native heritage—to turn us into people of compassion and love. What are some of the ways you have encountered God through your own traditions?

- What are some of the times others have shown you kindness and it changed your life?

- Think of some of the times you have experienced God's kindness, and write about them. What can you do to share kindness with others?

Notes

Introduction

1. Stasi Elredger, "Joy Is Meant to Be Ours," October 1, 2018, https://www.ransomedheart.com/blogs/stasi/joy-meant-be-ours.

2. Quoted in Evelyn Underhill, *Mysticism* (Stilwell, KS: Digireads.com, 2005 edition), 132.

1. On Tiptoe with Awe

1. "God's Grandeur" in *Poems of Gerard Manley Hopkins,* ed. by Robert Bridges (London: Humphrey Milford, 1918), 26.

2. Mike Cosper, *Recapturing the Wonder: Transcendent Faith in a Disenchanted World* (Westmont, IL: InterVarsity Press, 2017), 10.

3. From Kenneth L. Woodward's introduction to *The Book of Miracles* by George Fox (New York: Simon & Schuster, 2000), as quoted by Philip Zaleski, "Signs from Above," in *New York Times* Book Review, August 27, 2000, https://archive.nytimes.com/www.nytimes.com/books/00/08/27/reviews/000827.27zaleskt.html.

2. Joy Is a Choice

1. Lonnie B. Combs and J.B.F. Wright, "Precious Memories, Unseen Angels" (1945), https://hymnary.org/text/precious_memories_unseen_angels#pagescans.

2. "Faith and Inculturation," *International Theological Commission, Vol. II, Texts and Documents 1986–2007.* (San Francisco: Ignatius Press, 2009), par 6.

3. Finding Joy in Sacramentality

1. Alice Christiana Thompson Maynell, *The Collected Poems of Alice Maynell* (New York: Charles Scribner's Sons, 1914), 67.

2. Pope Benedict XVI, *Sacramentum Caritatis,* February 22, 2007, 70.

3. Kathleen R. Fischer, *The Inner Rainbow: The Imagination in the Christian Life* (New York: Paulist Press, 1983), 7.

4. Avery Dulles, "The Symbolic Structure of Revelation," *Theological Studies* 41, no. 1 (March 1980), 55–56.

4. Finding Joy in Eternity

1. St. Maria Faustina Kowalska, *Diary: Divine Mercy in My Soul* (Stockbridge, MA: Association of Marian Helpers, 2001), para. 777.

5. Finding Joy in Pain and Loss

1. The belt was not mine to keep—the Cherokee are a matrilineal society, and after Pop's death it was handed on from one generation to the next on the Native side of his family. Nevertheless, that little bonding ritual remains one of my most precious memories of my grandfather, Pop.

2. This thirteenth-century hymn known as the *Stabat Mater* is traditionally associated with both the feast of the Seven Sorrows (September 15) and the Stations of the Cross. Translated into English from the Latin by Edward Caswall (d. 1878).

6. Finding Joy in Singing with the Angels

1. *St. Augustine: City of God,* Books XVII–XXII, trans. Gerald G. Walsh and Daniel J. Honan (Washington, DC: Catholic University of America Press, 1954), 448.

2. "A whoop is an unspeakable joy which cannot be kept silent yet cannot be expressed because it surpasses comprehension." See Joseph A. Komonchak, "Whooping to the Lord," *Commonweal,* January 11, 2012, https://www.commonwealmagazine.org/whooping-lord.

3. Komonchak, "Whooping to the Lord."

4. Komonchak, "Whooping to the Lord," quoting Augustine's *On Psalm 46:1.*

5. One of the more beautiful accounts of this is Thomas of Celano's account of a Christmas Eve celebration in Greccio. Men and women from

all over the region came to join the friars to celebrate the wonder of the birth of the Savior. A manger scene with a crib was made, and the large crowd jubilated all night. In *The Life of St. Francis*, Thomas of Celano describes this tender and exuberantly joyful celebration of the birth of the Savior: "A manger has been prepared, hay has been brought, and an ox and an ass have been led up to the place. . . . The people arrive, and they are gladdened with wondrous delight at the great mystery. The woods resound with their voices and the rocks re-echo their jubilations. The friars sing and give due praise to the Lord, and all the night rings with jubilation. The saint of God (Francis) stands before the manger, sighing, overwhelmed with devotion and flooded with ecstatic joy. The sacrifice of the Mass is celebrated over the manger, and the priest experiences a new consolation." For more documentation on other instances of Francis and the early Franciscans praying this way, see my book *Sounds of Wonder* (New York: Paulist Press, 1977), 70–76.

6. I have included the Latin: "Ebrius amore et compasione Christi beatus Franciscus quandeque talia faciebat; nam dulcissima melodia spiritus intra ipsum ebulliens frequenter exterius gallicum dabat sonum; et vena divini susurrii quam auris ejus suscipiebat furtive, gallicum erumpebat in jubilum." *Fratre Leone, Speculum Perfectionis*, ed. Paul Abatier (Paris: Librairie Fischabcher, 1898), cap. 93.

7. For more information about this, see John Poirier's exciting book *The Tongues of Angels: The Concept of Angelic Languages in Classical Jewish and Christian Rites* (Mohr Siebeck, 2010).

8. Augustine, *Ennar. in Ps. 97*, 4; PL 37, 1272, trans. Abbott David Geraets, O.S.B.

9. Augustine, *City of God*, Book XXII, chapter 8.

10. *Albert and Thomas: Selected Writings*, ed. Simon Tugwell, Classics of Western Spirituality (New York: Paulist Press, 1998), 380.

11. Bernard Gui, "The Life of St. Thomas Aquinas," ed. and trans. Kenelm Foster, O.P., contained in *The Life of St. Thomas Aquinas: Biographical Documents* (Baltimore: Helicon Press, 1959), 38.

12. Thomas of Celano, *Early Franciscan Classics* (Paterson, NJ: St. Anthony Guild Press, 1962), 130.

13. Thomas of Celano, *St. Francis of Assisi: First and Second Life of St. Francis with Selections from the Treatise on the Miracles of Blessed Francis*, trans. Placid Hermann (Chicago: Franciscan Herald Press, 1963), 69.

14. Albert Seay, *Music in the Medieval World* (Englewood Cliffs, NJ: Waveland Press, 1965), 39.

15. Theodore Gerold, *Les Peres de l'Eglise et la Musique* (Paris: Etudes d'Histoire et de Philosophic Religieuse), 122.

16. *I Fioretti di San Francisco (Little Flowers of St. Francis),* second edition, edited by Prof. R. Fornaciari (Florence: Barbère, 1902), 51. Translated from the Italian by Deacon Eddie Ensley PhD and Fr. Douglas Kent Clark, STL. "Frate Masseo rimase pieno di tanta grazia della desiderata virtude della umilta e del lume di Dio, che d'allora innanzi egli era sempre in giubbilo: e spesse volte quando egli orava, facea un giubbilo in forma d'uno suono, a modo di Colombo, ottuso, U U l): e con faccia lieta, e cuore giocondo istava cosi in contemplazione; e con questo, essendo divenuto umilissimo, si riputava minore di tutti gli uomini del mondo. Domandato da Frate Jacopo da Fallerone, perche nel suo giubbilo egli non mutava verso, ripuose con grande letizia; che quando in una cosa si truova ogni bene, non bisogna mutare verso." See also Gianluigi Pasquale, *Day by Day with St. Francis* (Hyde Park, NY: New City Press, 2011), 131.

17. Marcelle Auclair, *St. Teresa of Avila* (New York: Pantheon Books, 1953), 221.

18. Auclair, *St. Teresa of Avila,* 222.

19. Auclair, *St. Teresa of Avila,* 222.

20. Auclair, *St. Teresa of Avila,* 222.

21. St. Peter Chrysologus, *Sermo VI in Ps. 99,* 6; PL 40, 680. For more information about this, see also my book *Sounds of Wonder* (New York: Paulist Press, 1977).

22. You can obtain more information about these seminars through Renewal Ministries (renewalministries.net).

23. Pope John XXIII, *Humanae Salutis,* December 25, 1961.

24. "Come, Creator Spirit," *Vatican News,* accessed January 24, 2020, https://www.vaticannews.va/en/prayers/come--creator-spirit.html.

7. Finding Joy in Scripture

1. This story about Aunt Genella was also shared in my *Messages from Heaven,* privately published.

2. Carl J. Arico, *A Taste of Silence* (New York: Continuum, 1999), 103.

3. Excerpt from *The Rule of St. Benedict,* chap. 4, accessed January 24, 2020, https://www.penguinrandomhouse.ca/books/172182/the-rule-of-saint-benedict-by-st-benedict/9780375700170/excerpt.

4. Fr. Luke Dysinger, O.S.B., "Accepting the Embrace of God: The Ancient Art of Lection Divina," accessed January 24, 2020, https://www.saintandrewsabbey.com/Lectio_Divina_s/267.htm.

5. Alexander MacLaren, D.D., "The Unwearied God and Wearied Man," accessed January 24, 2020, https://biblehub.com/sermons/auth/maclaren/the_unwearied_god_and_wearied_men.htm.

6. The section on the steps of lectio divina is also shared in my book *Step by Step Spirituality for Deacons* (Abbey Press, 2014).

8. The Joy of Conversing with God as a Friend

1. Michael F. Steltenkamp, *Nicholas Black Elk: Medicine Man, Missionary, Mystic* (Norman, OK: University of Oklahoma Press, 2017), chap. xx, Kindle.

2. *Alphonsus de Ligouri: Selected Writings*, Classics of Western Spirituality, ed. Frederic M. Jones (Mahwah, NJ: Paulist Press, 1999), 271–291.

3. *Liguori Selected Writings*, 284.

4. Edward M. Hallowell, *Worry* (New York: Pantheon Books, 1998), 63.

9. Finding Joy in Contemplative Prayer

1. Fr. Lawrence Lovasik, S.V.D., *Blessed Kateri Tekawitha: The Lily of the Mohawks* (Charlotte, NC: Catholic Book Publishing Company, 2012), 21.

2. Blaise Pascal, *Pensées* (New York: Penguin Books, 1966), 75.

3. Bernard of Clairvaux, *Sermons on the Song of Songs,* translated by Kilian Walsh, OCSO and Irene M. Edmonds, Vol. 1. (Collegeville, MN: Cistercian, 1971), Sermon 15, par 6.

4. *The Way of a Pilgrim and The Pilgrim Continues His Way*, ed. Faith Annette Sand, trans. Reginald Michael French (Pasadena, CA: Hope Publishing House, 1989), 29.

10. Finding Joy in Compassion

1. Isaac of Nineveh as quoted in K. M. George, *The Silent Roots: Orthodox Perspectives on Christian Spirituality* (Geneva: World Council of Churches Publications, 1994), 62–65.

2. Eduardo Aguero, "From Intimacy to Compassion" (academic paper, Creighton University, 2005), 37.

3. Pope John Paul II, Address at the Meeting with the Native Peoples of the Americas in Phoenix, September 14, 1987, 4, emphasis added, http://w2.vatican.va/content/john-paul-ii/en/speeches/1987/september/documents/hf_jp-ii_spe_19870914_amerindi-phoenix.html.

4. Deganawida was a great leader of Native peoples, who with Hiawatha founded the League of the Iroquois. Although Deganawida was the visionary, Hiawatha presented the message to the people because of Deganawida's speech impediment. In time he was named among the chiefs of the Iroquois Nation and worked to establish "The Great Peace." See "Deganawida," *Encyclopedia of World Biography, Encyclopedia.com*, accessed August 9, 2019, https://www.encyclopedia.com/history/encyclopedias-almanacs-transcripts-and-maps/deganawida.

Eddie Ensley is a permanent deacon in the Diocese of Savannah. He serves on the clergy staff at St. Anne Catholic Church in Columbus, Georgia. Ensley teaches graduate school at Josephinum Diaconate Institute, Pontifical College Josephinum, where he also serves as a course developer. He is a mission member of Alleluia Community, an ecumenical covenant community.

He and Robert Herrmann operate Deacons in Ministry, through which they have preached to more than 370,000 people in 350 locations since 2001. The two are coauthors of *Writing to Be Whole.*

Ensley is a licensed clinical pastoral counselor with a master's degree in pastoral studies (Loyola University) and a doctorate in clinical pastoral counseling (Cornerstone University). The author of fifteen books, he has more than thirty years of experience leading parish missions, retreats, and renewals.

Ensley is an enrolled member of the Echota Cherokee tribe and a member of the Knights of Columbus. He lives in Fortson, Georgia.

Robert Herrmann is a permanent deacon in the Diocese of Savannah. He serves on the clergy staff at St. Anne Catholic Church in Columbus, Georgia. An expert in spiritual journaling and teaching contemplative prayer, Herrmann is the coauthor of *Writing to Be Whole.*

Herrmann is certified in parish ministry from Loyola University. He has more than thirty years of experience leading parish missions, retreats, and renewals. He also served as campus minister and theology teacher at St. Anne-Pacelli Catholic School in Columbus.

Herrmann is a member of the Knights of Columbus. He lives in Fortson, Georgia.

Parishmission.net

Facebook: Deacon Robert Herrmann

Invite Deacons in Ministry to Your Parish, Retreat, or Conference

For decades Deacon Eddie Ensley and Deacon Robert Herrmann have preached to more than 370,000 people at parish missions, retreats, and conferences in more than 350 locations. People are reconciled. Faith is awakened. Vocations are discovered.

Here is what one pastor had to say about the event the deacons held at his parish:

"The mission proved to be a tremendous help for our families.... Our attendance was better than ever. The guided meditations throughout were vivid and uplifting. The parish mission was filled with solid content."
—Fr. John T. Euker
St. John the Baptist Parish, Perryopolis, Pennsylvania

The deacons can also lead clergy retreats and conferences as well as religious education conferences.

For more information about Deacons in Ministry and to view a parish mission video, visit **parishmission.net** or email Deacon Ensley at **pmissions@charter.net**.